PRESENTING
Barbara Wersba

Twayne's United States Authors Series
Young Adult Authors

Patricia J. Campbell, General Editor

TUSAS 698

Barbara Wersba. *Courtesy of Barbara Wersba*

PRESENTING

Barbara Wersba

Elizabeth A. Poe

Twayne Publishers
An Imprint of Simon & Schuster Macmillan
New York

Prentice Hall International
London Mexico City New Delhi Singapore Sydney Toronto

Twayne's United States Authors Series No. 698

Presenting Barbara Wersba
Elizabeth A. Poe

Twayne Publishers
An Imprint of Simon & Schuster Macmillan
1633 Broadway
New York, NY 10019

Library of Congress Cataloging-in-Publication Data

Poe, Elizabeth Ann.
    Presenting Barbara Wersba / Elizabeth A. Poe.
        p.   cm.— (Twayne's United States authors series ; TUSAS 698.
    Young adult authors)
        Includes bibliographical references (p.   ) and index.
        ISBN 0-8057-4154-2 (acid-free paper)
        1. Wersba, Barbara—Criticism and interpretation. 2. Young adult
    fiction, American—History and criticism.   I. Title.   II. Series:
    Twayne's United States authors series ; TUSAS 698.   III. Series:
    Twayne's United States authors series.   Young adult authors.
    PS3573.E69Z82   1998
    813'.54—dc21
                                                                    97-44279
                                                                    CIP

This paper meets the requirements of ANSI/NISO Z39.48–1992 (Permanence of Paper).

10 9 8 7 6 5 4 3 2 1

Printed in the United States of America

For Trevor and Ryan—
may you find and follow your dreams.

Contents

Contents

Foreword

The advent of Twayne's Young Adult Author Series in 1985 was a response to the growing stature and value of adolescent literature and the lack of serious critical evaluation of the new genre. The first volume in the series was heralded as marking the coming-of-age of young adult fiction.

The aim of the series is twofold. First, it enables young readers to research the work of their favorite authors and to see them as real people. Each volume is written in a lively, readable style and attempts to present in an attractive, accessible format a vivid portrait of the author as a person.

Second, the series provides teachers and librarians with insights and background material for promoting and teaching young adult novels. Each of the biocritical studies is a serious literary analysis of one author's work (or one subgenre within young adult literature), with attention to plot structure, theme, character, setting, and imagery. In addition, many of the series writers delve deeper into the creative writing process by tracking down early drafts or unpublished manuscripts by their subject authors, consulting with their editors or other mentors, and examining influences from literature, film, or social movements.

Many of the contributing authors of the series are among the leading scholars and critics of adolescent literature. Some are even YA novelists themselves. Each study is based on extensive interviews with the subject author and an exhaustive study of his or her work. Although the general format is the same, the individual volumes are uniquely shaped by their subjects, and each brings a different perspective to the classroom.

The goal of the series is to produce a succinct but comprehensive study of the life and art of every leading YA writer, as well as to trace how that art has been accepted by readers and critics, and to evaluate its place in the developing field of adolescent literature. And—perhaps most important—to inspire a reading and re-reading of this quality fiction that speaks so directly to young people about their life experiences.

PATRICIA J. CAMPBELL, General Editor

Preface

As I ride the Jitney bus from New York City to the east end of Long Island, drinking the juice our hostess has served, I surmise that most of the passengers are traveling to the Hamptons for the long Memorial Day weekend. Many, I suspect, live and work in the city during the week and relax in their Water Mill, North Haven, or Sag Harbor homes every weekend. Others may be vacationing in this popular resort area. Some, like myself, will be visiting for the day and returning on the evening bus. I have not been to the Hamptons before, but feel I have traveled there many times while reading Barbara Wersba's novels. I am approaching familiar territory. I have not met Barbara Wersba either, but her books tell me she is sensitive, intelligent, and compassionate. I have already formed a literary bond with her. When I arrive, I am greeted by Wersba and her friend Zue. We drive to Wersba's home in North Haven, where I am intrigued by her writing studio, the art and artifacts in the house, and the seclusion offered by the nearby woods and bay.

After lunch we tour the area and Wersba points out buildings, businesses, landscapes, and neighborhoods that serve as prototypes for places and settings in her Sag Harbor novels. I recognize many of them. This does not surprise me, because I have already toured Zürich, Switzerland, on the strength of Wersba's descriptions, and I'm in the process of doing the same in New York City. I enjoy imagining Wersba's characters in the settings in which she envisions them; having her for a guide is wonderful. But we don't just visit places. Wersba also introduces me to people who are important to her. I meet one of her writing students, who tells me how Wersba helps her discover herself through writing. I speak with the bookstore owner who Wersba fondly declares can locate any book she ever needs. I say hello to the waiter in the hotel where Wersba's characters often dine. And I am fortunate to have an extended dinner conversation with Wersba's longtime friend Zue. Throughout all this, Wersba is kindly answering my many questions, helping me piece together the fascinating pattern of her life and work.

I am indebted to Wersba for the day I spent with her in North Haven and our subsequent telephone conversations. I am also grateful to her for sharing her book reviews, photographs, letters, files, and latest manuscript. I appreciate, in addition to the travel itineraries she has provided me, the literary tangents my research on her has afforded. Thanks to Wersba, I have an enhanced appreciation for the artistic contributions of actress Eva Le Gallienne, New Zealand writer Janet Frame, choreographer and dancer Martha Graham, and the English poet Rupert Brooke. I have also enjoyed watching many of the old films she mentions in her books. But most of all I thank Barbara Wersba for her openness and willingness to cooperate. She has been most generous with her time and interest. As I suspected from her novels, she is a unique individual, and I am honored to have been given the opportunity to learn about (and from) her. I would also like to thank Charlotte Zolotow and William Morris of HarperCollins for their help and encouragement with this project. As Wersba's friend and former editor, Charlotte Zolotow was instrumental in arranging my visit with Wersba. My luncheon interview with this renowned author and editor was particularly helpful and enjoyable. Bill Morris, as always, was exceptionally supportive. I appreciate his providing me access to Wersba's review files.

I would like to acknowledge financial support for this project from the University of Wisconsin–Eau Claire and Radford University, both of which provided me grants and student help. I extend my thanks to the many students who have assisted in various aspects of the research for this book. I have enjoyed working with you all. I owe Patty Campbell a great debt for her patience and expertise. And as always, I thank my husband and our twin sons for their support.

Chronology

1965   *A Song for Clowns* published; opens country store in Palisades, New York

1966   *Do Tigers Ever Bite Kings?* published; begins reading to Carson McCullers

1968   *The Dream Watcher* published

1970   *Run Softly, Go Fast* published

1971   *Let Me Fall Before I Fly* published

1972   Meets Eva Le Gallienne

1973   *Amanda, Dreaming* published

1975   *The Country of the Heart* published; *The Dream Watcher* opens at the White Barn Theatre in Westport, Connecticut

1976   *Tunes for a Small Harmonica* published

1977   Receives honorary doctorate from Bard College; teaches at New York University

1978   *The Dream Watcher* opens in Seattle; forms the Women's Writing Workshop

1979   Teaches writing at Rockland Center for the Arts

1980   *Twenty-six Starlings Will Fly through Your Mind* published

1982   *The Carnival in My Mind* published; *The Crystal Child* published

1983   Moves to North Haven

1986   *Crazy Vanilla* published

1987   *Fat: A Love Story* published; *Love Is the Crooked Thing* published

1988   *Beautiful Losers* published; *Just Be Gorgeous* published; Barbara's mother dies

1989   *Wonderful Me* published

1990   *The Farewell Kid* published; *The Best Place to Live Is the Ceiling* published

1992   *You'll Never Guess the End* published

1994   *Life Is What Happens While You're Making Other Plans* published; Wersba opens her own small-press publishing company, The Bookman Press; publishes *A Tribute to Zue Sharkey*

1997   *Whistle Me Home* published; The Bookman Press publishes George Sand's *The Wings of Courage,* as retold by Barbara Wersba

1998   The Bookman Press publishes *At the New Year: A Poem by Kenneth Patchen*

1. Barbara Wersba: Loner, Actress, Writer, Teacher, Publisher, Friend

From the deck of her home in North Haven, Barbara Wersba can watch the blue herons as they swoop from the tall birches, locusts, and pines bordering her yard into the reeds and rushes beneath. She can see foxes and squirrels darting among the wildflowers and bushes surrounding her lawn. Occasionally, she can glimpse white-tailed deer or raccoons that have wandered in from the woods. Swans and geese frequently hold her gaze as they glide on the saltwater pond at the edge of the yard. Binoculars allow her to view great white egrets perching in the trees on the farside of the pond, and a zoom lens enables her to photograph them. Beyond the pond lies the harbor where she can see sailboats drift across the horizon. It's the type of place to inspire one to write—to imagine a boy and a girl, both loners, who inadvertently meet as they photograph swans. It's not surprising that many of the places in and around Sag Harbor and North Haven—the pond, the ferryboat, the old church, the ice-cream parlor, the hotel, the quiet residences, and the crowded summer streets—figure in Barbara Wersba's writing. In fact, the places she sees daily in her village on the eastern end of Long Island form backdrops for many of her young adult novels.

When she writes, Wersba works in the attic/studio of her North Haven home. She sits at a large, wooden craftsman's table, which she bought for 10 dollars and has used since she began writing 35 years ago. Her spacious, skylight-lit studio has an entire wall lined with built-in bookcases holding Wersba's library. She takes meticulous care of her books and has carefully arranged them according to the relationships of their authors: those whose authors were intimate stand next to each other; those whose authors were friends share the same shelf; and those whose authors did not get along occupy opposite ends of the bookcase. Framed enlargements of her original color photographs of wildflowers and birds keep her company in her study, as do mementos from the play she wrote for the famous actress Eva Le Gallienne and copies of the more than 25 books—many of which have been translated into foreign languages—she has written for children and young adults. Through the large window, Wersba can see the woods beside her house. The environment she has carefully created in her writing studio speaks clearly of her love for both the natural and the literary worlds.

In the tranquility of her studio, Wersba drafts her manuscripts on an IBM electric typewriter. She writes daily, preferring to begin at five o'clock in the morning, when she knows it will be quiet. She writes for about six hours each morning and then uses her afternoons in a variety of ways. When she is deeply involved in a book, she returns to work on it in the late afternoon. Otherwise she may read, garden, visit a friend or student, or walk along the bay beach. Wersba is always working on something, but not every manuscript is published. She estimates that for every success there are several failures. Wersba does not reject her failures, however, but carefully stores them in a trunk labeled "In Progress," which sits in a corner of the studio.

Wersba describes herself as a slow writer who casts every sentence many, many times when she is creating narrative. She compares writing her sentences to building a brick wall, and "if some of the bricks are weak, I can't build the wall."[1] As the sentences build upon one another, she frequently stops to read her words aloud, checking their coherence, their cadence, their flow, making sure the structure of these linguistic bricks is solid before she continues. She leaves wide margins for handwritten corrections and revises each page before she goes on to the next. When she has made changes in ink on several pages, she retypes those pages and may even revise them again. In six or seven hours, she may complete a maximum of three typewritten pages of narrative. Dialogue comes more quickly to her because she hears the characters talking in her mind and records their conversation as rapidly as possible. Therefore, she can go much further without revising. When a draft of the entire manuscript is completed, Wersba shows it to Betty Lee, her trusted friend who has excellent critical judgment and has been reading her manuscripts for many years. After taking Betty Lee's comments into account, Wersba sends the manuscript to her agent for further commentary.

Wersba has had four editors thus far, all prominent figures in the publishing world. She worked first with Jean Karl at Atheneum, then briefly with Ursula Nordstrom at Harper and Row until she retired, and then with Charlotte Zolotow until she retired as well. She now works with Marc Aronson, a senior editor at Henry Holt. Wersba has always had cordial relations with her editors, but her relationship with Charlotte Zolotow was very special. Reflecting on their work together, Wersba explains:

> I was completely in tune with Charlotte, and she with me because we're similar people. Under the safe umbrella of Charlotte's editorship I wrote 10 young adult novels within 12 years because she gave me a loving environment in which to work. She offered wonderful suggestions, and then she'd step back and let me go my own way. Probably the most sensitive editor I've worked with is Charlotte.[2]

The appreciation of their relationship is mutual. Charlotte Zolotow describes Wersba as an intense, sensitive person with a strong vision in her writing who takes suggestions seriously, studying them carefully before making changes. She admires Wersba's modesty and the close attention she pays to details in all that she does. Zolotow firmly believes Wersba has not received the recognition she deserves, and she is disappointed that Wersba has not been as financially successful as many lesser writers. Along with their excellent working relationship, Zolotow and Wersba developed a close friendship. They speak regularly on the telephone now that Zolotow no longer edits.[3]

The ideas for Wersba's books frequently come from a phrase that floats into her mind, sometimes well before she begins writing the book. She writes the phrase down, tacks it above her desk, and waits for the story behind the phrase to emerge. For example, the words "let me fall before I fly," which ran through Wersba's mind for many months, inspired Wersba to write the story of a child who finds a tiny circus parade in his backyard. In the early part of her career, Wersba was a very organized writer, relying heavily on research and detailed outlines to capture the emerging story. That is how she wrote her second through fifth children's stories. Her first young adult novel, however, did not follow the same approach. That book seemed to dictate itself to her from the depths of her subconscious, the story unfolding while she listened and typed. As she gained more experience writing, Wersba learned to rely on her first method, to wait and open herself to the story. Confident that the story will evolve, she now outlines only brief sketches of a book's beginning and ending. As ideas come to her, she makes little notes to herself on scraps of paper, on the backs of envelopes, and on the blackboard in the kitchen. When the book is finished, the phrase that originally inspired her usually becomes the title of the book.

The story inspired by the provocative phrase is shaped by many influences. Because everything she writes is personal, particular places and people sometimes demand to be part of the story. Therefore, although the Sag Harbor area serves as the setting for several of her more recent novels, other places she has lived or visited, along with people she has known or wondered about, frequently figure in her work. Wersba, like many writers of young adult fiction, draws heavily on past as well as current personal experiences to craft her novels. As she explains it, all her experiences and emotions become part of a great stew continually bubbling in a cauldron; each book represents a dip into the cauldron. But just like a stew's ingredients, life experiences get all mixed up, making each book a combination of what is happening in her life. Even the smallest things add flavor. Although the original experiences are generally transformed as they become part of fictional works, the emotions remain pure. For Wersba, the feelings are the essence of the story.

Barbara Wersba was born 19 August 1932. Her paternal grandfather, Max Wersba, was a Russian Jew who came to New York around the turn of the century with his brother from Riga, Latvia, where they had been tailors. Although the Wersba brothers came to America impoverished, they both made fortunes as Seventh Avenue clothiers. As Max gained financial success, he brought his young wife, Eda, and her relatives, one by one, to America. The extended Wersba family—the old grandmother, the aunts, the uncles—all lived in a brownstone in what is now Harlem but was in those days a white middle-class neighborhood. Barbara's grandparents had three children: Louis, Gertrude, and Robert. This prosperous family always had at least one maid and a nanny for the children. Max Wersba, who later committed suicide, was a strict, authoritarian parent. He did not want his children out on the street with the rough boys, so he had the top floor of the brownstone converted into a playroom with a pool table and a soda fountain. The children were always dressed in immaculate clothing.

But affluence did not protect the Wersbas from anti-Semitism. Robert, in particular, was conscious of prejudice, although both brothers tried hard to assimilate into mainstream American culture. Because marrying outside the Jewish faith seemed one way to become "less Jewish" as well as to gain social status, Louis and Robert both married gentile women. Louis married Natalie Mann, a beautiful Broadway actress who was divorced and had a child named Carolyn. Robert Wersba married Josephine Quarles, a Kentucky Baptist. The story of their meeting is unusual.

In the 1920s there was a real-estate boom in Florida. Because one could sell real estate without a license, many people rushed to Florida hoping to get rich selling land that would be developed into resort communities. Robert Wersba, then a young, handsome New Yorker in his late 20s, was in Florida trying to make his fortune when he met and began to date a charming, older woman named Susan Farmer Hampton, who was doing the same thing.

Susan had no interest in whether Robert was Jewish or not. They enjoyed each other's company and Robert frequently took her out to dinner. Finally she said to him, "I have a beautiful young daughter," and introduced him to Josephine, who was just barely 20. Robert and Josephine were soon deeply in love. Josephine was from a "shabby, genteel southern family that could have stepped out of Tennessee Williams." She and her mother were refined, southern women with beautiful manners who grew up poor in a family susceptible to alcoholism. Following his own father's example, Josephine's father deserted his family when she was quite young. Josephine's mother, Susan, was generally away from home trying to earn a living, so Josephine was brought up by her maternal grandmother. Grandmother Farmer was a tight-lipped, thin, puritanical Baptist who had been alive during the Civil War. Ever the rebellious child, Josephine ran off as a teenager and got married. The family had that marriage annulled instantly. Josephine's marriage to Robert Wersba lasted longer but also ended bitterly.

Josephine and Robert were married in Chicago in 1926. Robert's mother, a traditional Jewish matriarch, violently opposed their marriage on religious grounds. The couple was living in Chicago when Barbara was born, but when she was three years old, they all moved to New York City because Robert had a serious kidney condition caused by an injury received when he was an ambulance driver in France during World War I. He ended up being hospitalized for two years. During this time Barbara and her mother stayed with Barbara's paternal uncle, Louis, her aunt Natalie, and her cousins Lois and Carolyn, on West End Avenue. Josephine worked as a model on Seventh Avenue because she had no other income.

After Robert was released from New York Hospital, he took a job as a salesman for Kayser Hosiery in San Francisco. So when Barbara was seven, she and her parents drove to California and set up housekeeping in San Mateo, a suburb of San Francisco. Robert worked his way up from salesman to executive, but because he was often away from home, Barbara remembers little about him from when she was growing up. What she does remember are her parents' violent arguments. When her father would leave for long periods of time after an argument, Barbara's maternal grandmother, whom Barbara called Mama Susie, would come from New York to stay with them. Although Josephine was a talented artist, fashion designer, and model, she did not pursue a career other than homemaking while they lived in California.

Barbara remembers herself as a somber child who, from the age of seven or eight, seldom smiled. Painfully shy, she was always uncomfortable at school and considered herself a misfit in social situations. In addition to her shyness, her appearance probably also set her apart from her peers. Disregarding the Shirley Temple look of the times, Josephine tightly braided Barbara's hair each morning and dressed her in kneesocks, oxfords, and dark woolen clothing, giving her the appearance, Wersba recalls, of a German refugee.[4] Barbara attended first through sixth grades at Baywood Public School and seventh and eighth grades at the Notre Dame Academy in nearby Belmont, California.

As a child, Barbara was a loner who spent many hours sitting in an almond tree in the backyard of their hilltop home, gazing at the faraway city of San Francisco. She also rode her bicycle, roller-skated, and climbed the frames of the new homes being built in her neighborhood. She spent many hours daydreaming, writing poems, and creating dramas for her dolls. She dreamed of becoming a musician, a dancer, a poet, or anything that would take her away from the sadness that permeated her life. Wanting to escape her loneliness, she often imagined herself aboard the trains she heard as she lay in bed at night.[5]

World War II figures strongly in her childhood memories, particularly as it was glamorized in war movies by stars such as Tyrone Power, Bette Davis, Joan Crawford, Greta Garbo, and Betty Grable. Intrigued by the idea of acting, Barbara, when she was eight or nine, decided she wanted to become a stage actress. Her first step toward this goal was to volunteer her services at the Hilbarn Theatre, a community theater near San Mateo. Eleven-year-old Barbara boldly offered to run errands, pass out programs, go for coffee, or do anything else needed, in return for being allowed to watch the rehearsals. The directors accepted her offer of apprenticeship, and soon she was seeing quality acting in plays by Eugene O'Neill, Chekhov, Ibsen, and Shakespeare. Before long they gave her the part of Masha in a Russian play called *Listen, Professor.* Barbara worked hard at acting, assiduously memorizing her lines and searching the library for background information. Although she soon discovered she did not really like acting because it made her frightened and nervous, Barbara believed she belonged in the world of the theater. Her decision to become a great actress had provided her a purpose in life, so that even though she remained a loner by nature, she no longer felt alone (Sarkissian, 294).

When Barbara was 12, she found herself on one of the trains she had fantasized about, heading for New York City. After many tumultuous years of marriage, her parents were getting a divorce. Barbara's father had left for good, their house and furniture had been sold, and her two cats had been put to sleep. Of all these losses, the death of her cats grieved Barbara the most. On the day her cats were taken away, she hid in the crawl space under the house and wept. Even then Barbara knew she loved animals more than people.

Robert Wersba remarried within a year and moved to Los Angeles. His new wife already had two daughters near Barbara's age. Barbara and her mother took a train east to live near relatives and some old friends. At first, the two of them stayed at the Taft Hotel in the Broadway theater district. Before doing anything else in New York, Barbara bought a ticket to a play. She had never heard of the play, its playwright, or the starring actress, but when the matinee performance of Tennessee Williams's *The Glass Menagerie* starring Laurette Taylor was over, Barbara was stunned. After that moving performance, she reaffirmed her vow to someday become an actress.

After a while, Mama Susie joined Barbara and her mother, and the three of them moved into a large apartment on East 92nd Street. Josephine and her mother quarreled frequently, and Barbara spent a lot of time during her early teenage years with her uncle, Louis, and his family, at both their West End Avenue apartment and their summer home in Connecticut. Her mother, however, rarely visited her ex-husband's relatives. Close in age, Barbara and Lois were practically sisters as well as best friends. Like his father, Louis was a successful clothier; he also had the same authoritarian approach to raising children. A cultured man who loved art, collected paintings, and played classical piano, Uncle Louis took Barbara and Lois to theater, concerts, opera, and ballet. He worshiped his wife, Natalie, pampered her, took her on European trips, and bought her exquisite clothing and jewelry.

The contrast between her parents' relationship and that of her aunt and uncle was as obvious to Barbara as were the financial discrepancies between the two households. Josephine received very little alimony, so she and Mama Susie worked as saleswomen at Lord and Taylor. Robert, however, did pay for Barbara to attend New York City prep schools. She attended the Gardner School for Girls on Fifth Avenue for one year. After that she attended the Hewitt School, also on the east side of Manhattan.

Barbara was a poor student, except when it came to writing. As she puts it, "I was not interested in anything but English, and I wrote well and read well. But I was terrible in math, geography, sciences, and languages. I think the only thing that got me through school was that I wrote very well" (Janeczko, 90). After school hours, Barbara was free to explore New York City. Fascinated by the striking differences between a large city and San Mateo, she thoroughly enjoyed New York's museums, opera, ballet, and seemingly countless bookstores. Her father's relatives, the Jewish side of the family, encouraged Barbara's cultural appreciation and development.

Still intent upon becoming an actress, Barbara would sit in the last row of theater balconies and take notes while great Broadway actresses like Lynn Fontanne, Katharine Cornell, and Eva Le Gallienne performed. Although Barbara watched each of them carefully, she was particularly enthralled with Eva Le Gallienne, who epitomized what Barbara later called "the steady pursuit of excellence in the theatre" (Sarkissian, 295). When she was 16, Barbara took acting classes at the Neighborhood Playhouse and studied dance with world-renowned dancer and choreographer

Martha Graham. Graham was a demanding teacher who stressed disciplined movements that appeared to be simple and spontaneous. As a student of Graham, Wersba shares a legacy with many varied and famous actors and dancers, including Gregory Peck, Woody Allen, Paul Taylor, and Madonna. Wersba worked diligently at preparing for her chosen career, even though she still did not enjoy acting and suffered from stage fright. Always a loner at heart, the social atmosphere of New York theater made her ill at ease. She continued to read, write stories and poems, and collect books, but considered these pursuits secondary to her acting endeavors.

Barbara was also uneasy as an adolescent in the late 1940s, but she did what girls at her prep school were expected to do. She wore wool blazers, bobby socks, and penny loafers; attended formal dances with boys from respectable homes; and went on well-chaperoned overnight dates at West Point. And through it all, Barbara and her mother fought with each other. They argued over the usual teenage issues: clothing, curfew, hairstyles, boys, dates, makeup. Barbara was headstrong and wanted a lot of freedom; her mother was controlling and possessive. Even though Mama Susie was a sweet, loving, generous person who tried to encourage her, Barbara barely noticed her support. Josephine dominated the household. Feeling "squashed and stifled living in this household of women, none of whom got along," Barbara was always trying to get away. The first time she did, however, was the summer before college, when she acted in summer stock.

During her adolescence, Barbara visited her father twice a year at his home in Beverly Hills, California. Robert Wersba had married a woman with money, so he and his new family lived in comfort. Their opulent lifestyle was a terrible contrast to the life her mother and grandmother lived on East 92nd Street in New York. Barbara's visits to her father were never happy, and she and her father were never close. Just as her mother would complain bitterly to Barbara about her father not paying enough alimony, her father would viciously criticize her mother. The acrimony between them was disillusioning for Barbara, who felt like a Ping-Pong ball between two people she wanted to look up to but could not.

When she graduated from prep school, her father wanted her to go to a prestigious college, preferably Vassar or Smith. Barbara, however, chose to apply to Bard, a small liberal-arts college where she could study drama. Her entrance exam was a stage audition. She went alone to the interview, performed a scene from George Bernard Shaw's *Saint Joan,* and was accepted. Ignoring her father, 18-year-old Barbara packed her trunks, left her mother's apartment, and moved to Bard College in Annandale-on-Hudson, New York.

Her decision proved advantageous. She thrived at Bard with its student body of 300 and faculty of young, enthusiastic professional artists from New York who taught students individually or in small seminars. Barbara took all the English courses possible, acted in all the college's plays, and learned everything she could about acting, directing, and stagecraft. She continued studying dance with Martha Graham and played the piano late into the night. At one point Barbara's father visited Bard and, disapproving of this progressive school devoted to the arts, which he described as a haven for beatniks, wanted her to withdraw. Fortunately, Aunt Natalie, "a great champion of [Barbara's] put her foot down and said this is the first really happy time this child has ever had, do *not* pull her out of college. She's doing well. Let her alone." Robert listened to his sister-in-law and continued to pay the school's tuition, but gave his daughter no other money. Barbara earned book and spending money by operating a traveling doughnut/coffee business in the dorms, tending the little college graveyard, baby-sitting, housecleaning, typing, and waitressing in the campus coffee shop.

During the summers she did summer stock at the Forestburgh Summer Theatre in the Catskills and the Arena Theatre in Orleans, Massachusetts; in the winter "field periods," she worked off-Broadway at the Provincetown Playhouse. She got the lead in so many plays at Bard, she became "the leading lady of the theater department." But although her life revolved around theater (she was a successful acting student whose friends and mentors were all actors), Barbara still did not enjoy acting and continued to be plagued by stage fright. As she had done as a child and a teen, she wrote stories during her free time, but her writing displeased her and she never completed a piece. Loving animals as she did, she generally kept a stray cat or two in her dorm room for company. As a college senior, Barbara considered applying for a Fulbright Scholarship to study acting in England. Uncertain as to whether this was a good idea, she followed an impulse and, although she had never met her, wrote Eva Le Gallienne, asking her advice. To her surprise, Miss Le Gallienne responded. She suggested Barbara study in her own country rather than abroad, and Barbara took her advice. In June 1954, a week after she graduated from Bard, Wersba began working with a stock company in Princeton, New Jersey. Wersba had the lead in every play the company performed, and after she opened as Marguerite Gautier, the legendary "Camille," in Tennessee Williams's *Camino Real,* José Quintero, a New York director, came backstage and said he had a part for her on Broadway. Although she knew she should have been elated, Wersba instead felt empty; she never followed up on the director's offer. In fact, she did not even finish the season. She had a "quiet nervous breakdown midseason because of too many years of struggle. It took a toll on [her] and [she] fell apart right after college."

About a year later, she moved to New York's Greenwich Village, where she took a cold-water flat in a tenement building on East Ninth Street. Once again her father was angry, this time because he believed girls should live at home until they married. In the Village, Barbara joined ranks with many other aspiring young actresses and actors as they made "the rounds." Making the rounds entailed visiting theatrical offices; trying, usually unsuccessfully, to talk with someone influential; and then leaving a photograph and résumé, knowing full well no one of any importance would ever look at them. Wersba's East Ninth Street tenement building was filled with many young hopefuls. The aspiring actresses living there shared the one good coat among them, a fur, as they made the rounds. Wersba found many of the building's tenants noteworthy. She recalls five-foot-tall Dennis who wanted to be an opera singer, harpist Samantha who had to keep her harp in the hall because her room was too small to hold it, and shady Beryl who had "a stream of gentleman callers" (Commire, 182). The building itself was intriguing. In a flat so small the bathtub was stored and used in the kitchen, Wersba painted the floors brick red, built bookcases from floor to ceiling, listened to Bach and Mozart on a beat-up phonograph, and read constantly while sitting in a straw chair with the sunlight streaming over the windowsill. Summers were stifling and winters were freezing. Rats and roaches were frequent uninvited guests, but stray cats were always welcome.

For the five years Wersba lived in Greenwich Village, she supported herself with a series of part-time jobs, some of them very odd. Jobs related to her field included performing as an extra on live dramatic television shows such as the *U.S. Steel Hour,* doing voice-over for commercials and cartoons, reading radio scripts, and performing off-Broadway. She also earned money by working as a clerk in bookshops and department stores, a projectionist for a film company, an office typist, a governess for the young son of a television personality, a mosaic maker, a waitress at Schrafft's, and the head of the correspondence department at a government housing agency.

While working these jobs, she attended the Paul Mann Actors Workshop three evenings a week. There she studied with excellent teachers such as Morris Carnofsky, who taught Shakespeare, and Lloyd Richards. It was an excellent acting school—of the Stanislavsky method. Having worked with Paul Mann in the late '50s, Wersba describes him as "a brilliant, temperamental teacher" who encouraged his students to form their own acting companies (Sarkissian, 298).

So as soon as they graduated, Wersba, in her middle 20s, and six of Mann's other students compiled a staged reading of famous stories about childhood, which they called *When I Was a Child.* In addition to performing, Wersba was responsible for adapting stories by people such as Dylan Thomas and Virginia Woolf for the stage. She found she thoroughly enjoyed the type of writing involved in converting narrative to drama. That winter the seven of them rented a Volkswagen bus; stuffed their suitcases, costumes, stage equipment, guitars, and themselves into it; and took the production on the road. For the next three months, they traveled across America, performing in college auditoriums and sleeping in dilapidated motels. Tired but enthusiastic, they returned to New York with plans to put the show on Broadway.

Wersba, however, left the company upon returning to New York and learning she had hepatitis. During her three-month convalescence at the home of her friend Betty Lee, on Martha's Vineyard, Wersba realized she did not want to return to the theater. Her life now lacked direction, but she was relieved to be rid of the responsibility that came with the goal she had set at such a young age. Her 15-year struggle, which had shown her the distressing, cruel, and frustrating side of the theater, was over. She had been a successful actress, but she would no longer devote her life to acting.

While Wersba recuperated, Betty Lee suggested she write something and provided her friend with paper, pen, and solitude. Inspired by the sea she had been watching for so long, Wersba spent the next few weeks writing. The result was a story called *The Boy Who Loved the Sea*. It was the first piece she had been able to finish, and she was proud of it. Although the story, a fantasy about a boy who goes to live in the sea, was clearly a children's story, Wersba had not set out to write for children and knew nothing about children's literature. She simply wrote the story as it came to her.

A few nights after the story was completed, Connie Campbell, the chief copy editor of the New York publishing house Coward-McCann (which is now Putnam's), came to a dinner party given by Betty Lee. Unbeknownst to Wersba, Betty Lee slipped the manuscript for *The Boy Who Loved the Sea* into Campbell's purse. After reading it, Campbell took it to Alice Torrey, the children's book editor at Coward-McCann, and said, jokingly, that she would quit if the story were not published. Torrey, who is remembered as an editor with excellent judgment who took chances and was not afraid to go out on a limb,[6] read the manuscript, liked it, and sent Wersba a note saying she would publish it.

In contrast to her struggle with acting, the ease with which she became a published writer gave Wersba pause. She still did not feel she wrote well but thought it possible to teach herself to write. She intuited that she possessed the temperament of a writer and believed she would find more joy in writing than she ever had in acting. The acknowledgment that she preferred the privacy writing allowed as opposed to the public show that acting demanded enabled her to begin her new career, at the age of 29, with enthusiastic determination.

About this time Wersba's father was hospitalized with cancer in Los Angeles. She flew out to visit him several times and spent many days by his bedside. His slow death upset her very much because they had never had a good relationship. Robert was a man who had never wanted a family. But as he lay in the hospital, Josephine wrote a beautiful letter for Barbara to read to him. In it Josephine told him how she had always admired him and what a brave man she thought he was. She thanked him for the many advantages he had given Barbara and encouraged him to hold on and live and enjoy his life. Barbara was deeply touched by this letter. It helped her realize that as tempestuous as her parents' relationship had been, they still loved one another. This was a comforting revelation because she had no happy memories of their marriage and had been disenchanted by their relationship since she was a small child.

Barbara had a similar revelation about the nature and depth of her mother's feelings when Mama Susie died. Josephine kept a vigil by the coffin and wept bitterly. Barbara was amazed at the intensity of her mother's love for Mama Susie, whom Josephine had constantly criticized. At the burial, when the coffin was lowered into the ground, Barbara thought her mother was going to jump into the grave. Even though Josephine and her mother had lived together off and on for all of Josephine's life, even after Josephine had remarried and moved to the Bronx while Barbara was in college, Josephine and Mama Susie fought. Yet, on some very deep level, Josephine loved and needed her mother and did not know how she would live without her.

Around the time Wersba's father was dying in 1961, *The Boy Who Loved the Sea,* illustrated by Margot Tomes, was published, and Campbell introduced Wersba to Pat Schartle, who became her agent, at McIntosh and Otis. Wersba promptly started work on her second children's book, *The Brave Balloon of Benjamin Buckley.* This book was more difficult to write, but Wersba persevered. When Wersba finished the manuscript, Pat Schartle recommended she submit it to Atheneum, a new publishing house. They accepted the manuscript and published it in 1963. Jean Karl edited this fantasy about ballooning in the eighteenth century, and Margot Tomes again illustrated. The *New York Times* reviewed *The Brave Balloon of Benjamin Buckley,* but the reviewer misunderstood the book. Wersba sent a letter to George Wood protesting the review and explaining what the book was about. Wood wrote back, offering her a position as a regular reviewer for the *New York Times Sunday Book Review.* The reviewer, whom Wersba prefers not to name, also wrote to her, suggesting they have lunch. They did and became fast friends. Over the course of 17 years, Wersba reviewed more than 100 books in the *New York Times Sunday Book Review.* In the meantime, knowing she wanted to continue writing children's books, but unfamiliar with the form, Wersba educated herself about the genre by reading numerous children's books and learning the differences among picture books, storybooks, and novels. With eight hours of hard work each day at the typewriter, Wersba produced her third children's book, *The Land of Forgotten Beasts,* which Margot Tomes illustrated and Atheneum published in 1964 and Gollancz of London published in 1965. This third fantasy involved mythical animals.

About the time *The Land of Forgotten Beasts* was published, Wersba moved from New York City to Rockland County, New York, where she shared a pre-Revolutionary house with Betty Lee in the artists' community of Snedens Landing. In the early 1960s, Betty Lee bought a 150-year-old building in Palisades, near Snedens Landing, which she and Wersba turned into an old-fashioned country store. To do this, they went all over New England researching what country stores were like in the 1800s. A number of talented local artists—painters and graphic designers—assisted in the transformation of the building, making it authentic Americana. Lee and Wersba stocked their Palisades Country Store with typical nineteenth-century wares: penny candy, tobacco, Vermont cheese, home-baked goods, jams and jellies, housewares, and toys. Wersba worked on her books in the mornings and tended the store in the afternoons. She also wrote advertising copy for the store in the afternoon sometimes. Their fascinating store was featured in magazines and on the NBC evening news. Artists and theatrical people living in Snedens Landing, such as Katharine Cornell, Gert Macy, and Ginger Rogers, would often bring their houseguests over to the store to browse and have a cup of coffee. Celebrities from New York, including Noel Coward and Mary Martin, also patronized the store. Wersba and Lee operated the country store for seven years. They eventually moved from their rented house into the store itself, slowly transforming it into a home.

Wersba's fourth children's book, *A Song for Clowns,* a tale of traveling medieval minstrels who rid a troubled world of its sorrows, illustrated by Mario Rivoli, was published by Atheneum in 1965 and by Gollancz in 1966. Mario Rivoli also illustrated Wersba's fifth children's book and first book of verse, *Do Tigers Ever Bite Kings?,* which Atheneum published in 1966. That same year, a friend asked Wersba if she would like to read to an invalid in the neighboring town of Nyack. Although reluctant, Wersba agreed to help. The invalid turned out to be Carson McCullers, and for the next several years Wersba visited her daily, becoming a surrogate member of her household. She read to, shopped for, ate with, and took dictation from this great southern writer who was almost completely paralyzed from a series of strokes.

Wersba admired McCullers greatly and they became dear friends. McCullers had such tremendous physical and emotional needs at this point in her life that she was egocentric. She would telephone Wersba in the middle of the night with ideas for novels or poems that she needed to have put in writing before they faded. They never discussed Wersba's writing, but Wersba found McCullers "inspiring because she was such a genius." Wersba gave to her unselfishly for two years, and she was with her when she died in Nyack Hospital in 1968.

Difficult as it was during this time, Wersba continued to write her own stories in the mornings. In 1967 she was working on her sixth book, a historical novel set in eighteenth-century London, when the voice of Albert Scully interrupted her. The voice of this young man was so insistent that she put the historical novel aside and spent the next seven months at the typewriter composing *The Dream Watcher*. In this first of Wersba's young adult novels, 14-year-old Albert Scully, a loner and misfit, develops an intense friendship with a beautiful old woman, Mrs. Orpha Woodfin, who lies when she tells him she has been a famous actress. The publication of *The Dream Watcher* by Atheneum in New York in 1968 and Longmans Young in London in 1969 changed Wersba's life. Not only did it sell well and make her reputation as one of the pioneers (along with S. E. Hinton, Paul Zindel, Ann Head, and Robert Lipsyte) in the newly defined genre called young adult literature, it would eventually connect her with the great Broadway actress she so admired, Eva Le Gallienne.

Writing *The Dream Watcher* also helped Wersba realize the important role older people had played as mentors in her life. As she puts it, "Most of the people in my life who have been of influence have been older. I seem to have had a tremendous need for parent figures, probably because I felt so unappreciated by my own parents." She strongly believes that children need adults to tell them they are special, good, talented, loved, bright—a type of nurturing she calls mirroring. Wersba didn't seem to get this from her parents so she was "starved to get it from teachers, theater directors, Eva Le Gallienne, Pat Schartle, Connie Campbell—all the people in [her] life." She remembers one particular English teacher at the Hewitt School, Mrs. Riggs, who nurtured her writing. At Bard College a wonderful theater director, Larry Wismer, greatly encouraged her in her acting. Paul Mann was an extremely helpful acting teacher. But besides these, Wersba remembers having had generally "very sensitive teachers all through [her] education and [considers herself] very lucky."

Wersba published another young adult novel, *Run Softly, Go Fast,* with Atheneum in 1970. This story, which revolved around the drug culture of the '60s, was also well received and won a major European book prize. She wrote two more children's books: *Let Me Fall Before I Fly* and *Amanda, Dreaming.* Both were published by Atheneum, in 1971 and 1973 respectively, and illustrated by Mercer Mayer. *Let Me Fall Before I Fly,* which is Wersba's favorite of all her books, is the story of a young child who discovers a miniature circus in the grass in his backyard. *Amanda, Dreaming* describes the wonderfully fantastic dreams Amanda experiences every night and shares with no one. In 1975 Atheneum published *The Country of the Heart,* an exploration of the relationship between a dying middle-aged poet and a teenage neophyte poet. Nearly 20 years later this novel would be made into a television movie entitled *Matters of the Heart,* starring Jane Seymour.

Throughout all this, interest in *The Dream Watcher* remained high. Readers continually wrote to express their strong identification with the novel's characters; film producers inquired about making it into a movie; and people still requested a sequel. Wersba, however, was anxious to move on to new books and did not take these comments seriously. Then the noted actress/director Margaret Webster called with a message that Wersba took quite seriously. Webster had given a copy of *The Dream Watcher* to Eva Le Gallienne, who had read it, liked it, and wanted to play the part of the old woman, Orpha Woodfin. And Eva Le Gallienne wanted to meet Barbara Wersba.

Wersba was mute with admiration when she first met the great actress in 1972 in Le Gallienne's Connecticut home. Although Miss Le Gallienne was an old woman now, the vitality of her personality and the richness of her voice remained. When she asked Wersba to write a play for her, all Wersba's plans for children's books and young adult novels vanished. Wersba modestly replied that she did not know how to write plays. Miss Le Gallienne advised her to learn, and Wersba, for the second time, took her advice.

Feeling that her life had come full circle at the age of 40, Wersba devoted the next seven years trying to realize Miss Le Gallienne's dream. She spent eight months immersing herself in dramatic form by reading two plays each morning and two plays each night. In the afternoons she worked on a stage version of *The Dream Watcher*. When she completed an act, she would take it to Miss Le Gallienne in Connecticut for comments and suggestions. Wersba carefully revised and with a year's worth of painstaking work, she transformed *The Dream Watcher* into a play.

During this year Wersba developed a strong friendship with the glamorous actress she had admired in her childhood. Le Gallienne, as Wersba already knew, was not only an actress:

> She was a Renaissance person; she could do anything. There was no form of art she could not practice. She was the Orson Welles of her day, in terms of theater. There's a parallel between her and Orson Welles. The movies didn't know what to do with him because he was a genius. Le Gallienne was also a genius, but the theater didn't know what to do with her after her Civic Rep [repertory theater] failed on Fourteenth Street. Her career really ended at age 32. She was the first woman actor/manager in America. No woman before that had ever had her own theater, acted, directed, and produced.

Le Gallienne also wrote children's books and translated fairy tales from Danish to English. Wersba and Le Gallienne discovered they had much in common. They were both self-recognized loners who loved animals, nature, and books. Miss Le Gallienne fed animals from the woods every night from her kitchen door and had a magnificent garden. She also had the finest library Wersba had ever seen (Sarkissian, 300). In addition, Wersba discovered a wonderful coincidence: Eloise Armen, Miss Le Gallienne's companion and secretary, had been backstage attending Laurette Taylor the afternoon 12-year-old Barbara Wersba had been mesmerized by *The Glass Menagerie*. Interestingly, Wersba never told Le Gallienne how deeply she had inspired her as a teenager.

The Dream Watcher opened in 1975 at the White Barn Theatre in Westport, Connecticut. It was a great success, and Wersba tasted the joy playwrights experience when the audience loves a play. Having passed its summer tryout, the next step was to prepare for what Wersba and Le Gallienne hoped would be a Broadway production. A new version of the play was to be produced in partnership with the Seattle Repertory Theatre and travel to cities like Boston and Philadelphia until it eventually reached Broadway. Wersba's play was revised, recast, and restaged. It opened in Seattle the winter of 1978 and was a disaster. All the changes had worked together to create a production quite unlike the one performed at the White Barn Theatre. In Wersba's estimation, the actor who played Albert Scully was too old, the director was insecure, the stage design was too elaborate, and she did not believe in the script revisions she had been asked to make (Sarkissian, 300). As Eva Le Gallienne put it when she called the cast together the following day, "Our butterfly has been cloaked in iron" (Sarkissian, 300). Having failed its out-of-town tryout, the play closed in a few weeks. Wersba returned to Palisades, New York, moved back into the country store, went to bed with her two cats, and slept.

The beauty and familiarity of the Palisades Country Store provided Wersba solace. Here, before the play, she had spent many mornings writing and worked as a storekeeper in the afternoons. Here, during the seven years she was involved with the play version of *The Dream Watcher,* Wersba had also written *Tunes for a Small Harmonica,* her fourth young adult novel, which Ursula Nordstrom edited, Harper and Row published in 1976, and The Bodley Head of London published in 1979. It was here, to the country store, she had returned after the many hours she spent reading to and caring for Carson McCullers. And here she had always taken in, befriended, and found homes for numerous stray animals. And so it was here, with the sun streaming through the stained-glass windows onto the marble countertops and the soft glow given off by the old-fashioned lamps, that Wersba returned to find comfort in her animals, her books, and her friends.

Reaching beyond the pain of the fiasco in Seattle, Wersba surprised herself by starting the Women's Writing Workshop. The Palisades Country Store had closed, and Betty Lee had moved

back to Martha's Vineyard, so Wersba took over the whole building. She held classes at first for 10 students. But as more and
more women joined, she increased the number of sessions she
offered. As she worked with these novice writers, Wersba soon
felt herself healing and functioning again. Guiding her students,
encouraging her students, and writing with them, she began to
understand her craft for the first time. Her writing changed,
becoming more natural, as she started to compose "from feeling
rather than expectation" (Sarkissian, 301). The following year
she gave classes at the Rockland Center for the Arts, a local cultural center, and in the summer she taught at New York University. As in the Women's Writing Workshop, the adults who
attended her classes wrote to discover truths about themselves
and their lives. Wersba did the same.

Wersba's next two books were children's books. Ursula Nordstrom had retired from Harper, and Charlotte Zolotow became
Wersba's editor. *Twenty-six Starlings Will Fly through Your
Mind,* an unconventional alphabet book illustrated by David Palladini, was published by Harper and Row in 1980. In 1982,
Harper published *The Crystal Child* (illustrated by Donna Diamond), a modern fairy tale in which a boy's love brings to life a
young girl who has been turned into a statue. Wersba originally
wrote this story as a gift for her friend Zue Sharkey. That same
year Harper and Row published Wersba's fifth young adult novel,
The Carnival in My Mind, the story of a neglected teenager whose
mother raises Irish setters. About this time Pat Schartle retired
from McIntosh and Otis, and Julie Fallowfield became Wersba's
agent.

In 1981, after she had completed the manuscript for *Carnival*
but before it was published, Wersba went to Switzerland with Zue
Sharkey. Zue, who had been a student in one of Wersba's writing
classes, was a UNICEF director for the United Nations. Zue was
an art expert, and her job was to create and expand the UNICEF
greeting-card line. She and Wersba traveled to Switzerland several times, but on one particular flight, they happened to sit next
to Marian Shaw. At the end of the plane ride, Mrs. Shaw asked
Wersba to send her a copy of one of her books. Wersba sent a copy

of *Carnival* to her. She and her husband, Irwin Shaw, liked Wersba's literary work so much they wanted to make a film with her. Wersba and Irwin Shaw collaborated on the screenplay for *Carnival* at the Shaws' summer home in Southampton, New York, on the east end of Long Island. Mr. Shaw died before the film came to fruition, but in the course of the collaboration, Wersba and Zue had discovered Sag Harbor. Wersba had a hunch she would like living there, so in 1983, when Betty Lee sold the country store, Wersba and Zue moved to Sag Harbor's sister village, North Haven.

The village of Sag Harbor was an important whaling town during the nineteenth century. It became a factory town in the early part of the twentieth century. Now it is one of a cluster of resort villages, called the Hamptons, popular with New York City dwellers. Sag Harbor's year-round residents include artists, writers, and the local families who own and operate Sag Harbor's hotels, shops, and services. West of town lies Morton National Wildlife Refuge, which encompasses a variety of natural habitats including ponds, beaches, and bluffs.

Upon moving to the Sag Harbor area, Wersba bought a camera and began photographing wildlife. Not surprisingly, her next young adult novel, *Crazy Vanilla,* published by Harper and Row in 1986, is set in North Haven and is the story of two teenage wildlife photographers. Wersba's next three young adult novels form a trilogy about Rita Formica, who lives in Sag Harbor and falls in love with Arnold Bromberg, a man twice her age. *Fat: A Love Story* and *Love Is the Crooked Thing* were published by Harper and Row in 1987, and *Beautiful Losers* was published by Harper and Row in 1988, the year Wersba's mother died.

When Barbara was in college, her mother had married Howard Tyson, a retired civil servant, and they lived in the Bronx. Barbara and her mother had never been emotionally close, but they did communicate regularly, and Barbara believes "she had become much more understanding of her mother in the last years of her life because [Barbara] was at last maturing." When her mother was in the hospital in the Bronx, Barbara made the three-hour bus and subway trip from Sag Harbor to visit her every 10 days. The night before Josephine died, Barbara called her mother in her hospital room and said she was coming to see her the next day. Then without thinking about it, she said, "I love you, Mother." Her mother, surprised, caught her breath and said, "Oh Barbara, I love you too." Barbara replied, "I'll see you tomorrow," and they both hung up. Two hours later, Barbara's mother died. She was 82 and wasted from diabetes. Barbara is convinced that by saying "I love you" she released her, "because I hadn't said that since I was a little girl. I hadn't said anything nice to my mother since I was a child. And some instinct, some higher power, allowed me to say 'I love you.' I believe I allowed her to die, and I was *very* glad I said it."

Soon after her mother's death, Wersba wrote a second trilogy, this time about Heidi Rosenbloom, a teenage misfit living on Manhattan's Upper East Side. The trilogy begins with *Just Be Gorgeous,* which was published in 1988. *Wonderful Me* came out in 1989, followed in 1990 by *The Farewell Kid.* Harper and Row published all three hardcover versions and Dell put them out in paperback. In 1990 HarperCollins published *The Best Place to Live Is the Ceiling,* which takes place mainly in Switzerland, and in 1992 published *You'll Never Guess the End,* which is set in New York City. About this time Charlotte Zolotow retired from Harper. Although Wersba and Zolotow remained close friends, they would no longer work together as author and editor.

It was also during this time that Barbara Wersba discovered the autobiography of Janet Frame, New Zealand's finest fiction writer. Awed by both the writing and the person, Wersba proceeded to read Frame's novels, short stories, and poems. She remained stunned and as she puts it, "I got a literary crush on her. So taking a big risk, I called her in New Zealand to tell her how profoundly her work had affected me." Wersba and Frame have since become great friends, talking on the phone weekly. Both are quite shy, and laugh at certain middle-age problems they share. Wersba's essay "On Discovering Janet Frame" attests to the personal significance Frame's work has held for her, as does Wersba's decision, induced by Frame's prose, to stop writing for a while and contemplate the relationship of her own life and her art. Wersba writes: "I needed to be still, that I might find a way to make deeper use of the past."[7] Wersba's next book, *Life Is What Happens While You're Making Other Plans,* the story of a boy who wants to be an actor and is encouraged by a New Zealand film star, was published in 1994 by The Bodley Head of London. Her latest book, *Whistle Me Home,* an unusual love story, was written under the editorship of Marc Aronson and was published in 1997 by Henry Holt and Company.

The serenity offered by her home in North Haven seems to suit Wersba and her writing. She has written 12 of her 16 young adult novels in the quietness of her writing studio, surrounded by reminders of important aspects of her life. In addition to her wildlife photography, Wersba has a photograph of Eva Le Gallienne performing in *The Dream Watcher;* the silver watering can she gave Miss Le Gallienne after opening night in Seattle; the glass-cube paperweight inscribed with *Dream Watcher,* which she gave Le Gallienne when they opened in Westport; and the love seat used in a stage production of *The Barretts of Wimpole Street,* starring Katharine Cornell, which Zue gave her. Her honorary doctoral degree from Bard College is framed and hangs on the wall along with playbills from *The Dream Watcher;* a poster from Davos, Switzerland; and artwork from the covers of her books.

Wersba also displays reminders of the past throughout the rest of the house. The large bean chest from the old country store in Palisades forms one side of the North Haven house's kitchen area. A gold horse's head also from the country store hangs from a wall in the living room. Artwork, books, and furniture are reminiscent of Zue, who died in the winter of 1994. Wersba speaks of Zue as "a fascinating and highly evolved human being" whom she "loved and admired tremendously." Wersba considers the 15 years she knew Zue to be the happiest years of her life. They did not live together all of those years, but in Wersba's judgment the "years in North Haven with Zue were the very best because I had a wonderful home and I produced 10 books." Reflecting on her productivity during these years, Wersba adds, "Zue provided me with a haven in which to write. And I think it was because of the lovely environment she created for both of us that I was able to write so many books. She was a very gentle, nurturing person." Wersba also nurtured Zue, who was 19 years her senior. Wersba had long been concerned about Zue's health and nursed her through many asthma attacks. But Zue did not make it through her final asthma attack, and she died in the arms of her beloved companion, Barbara. Zue's death was a tremendous loss to Wersba.

Once again to help her through a painful time, Wersba reached out to others by teaching writing. In the fall of 1994, she began holding classes for women in her attic writing studio. She had also worked with individual students from time to time, one of whom, Lynn Lauber, published an important novel called *White Girls,* but at this point Wersba sought the warmth and companionship she had found previously with groups of women seeking to discover themselves. Meeting in her studio, Wersba's 15 students led Wersba into another phase of her life. She notes that now that she is older, she has become a mentor to her students, which is funny to her because it had always been her role to be everybody's child.

Wersba did not write for nearly two years after Zue's death, but in the summer of 1995 she began work on another novel. But even before Zue's death, Wersba was beginning to seriously question the direction her writing would take. The influence of Janet Frame and the loss of Charlotte Zolotow as her editor had much to do with these questions, but so did changes in New York publishing houses. For years, she had been watching with dismay as smaller houses were bought up by large conglomerates. With fewer houses to submit manuscripts to, authors, particularly new ones, were having difficulty getting published. Growing less and less inclined to take risks, the large publishing houses seemed primarily interested in surefire moneymakers. Literary quality and creativity no longer seemed to be as important as they once were. So Wersba decided to make a significant change in her life and joined the small-press movement: she started her own publishing company, The Bookman Press.

On 8 March 1994, The Bookman Press published its first book, *A Tribute to Zue Sharkey.* Zue's book contains essays, poems, and letters from people around the world. It, like the others Wersba plans, is a limited-edition chapbook printed by letterpress on fine paper and bound between marbled covers. *A Tribute to Zue Sharkey* was planned as a surprise for Zue's 80th birthday, but she died before it was completed. Copies of this exquisite little volume were given to people at the UN and elsewhere who had known and loved this remarkable woman.

Sometimes various aspects of Wersba's life converge, or as she puts it, life comes full circle. This happened when she began to turn her experiences as a lonely, imaginative child into stories published for children and young adults. It also happened when actress Eva Le Gallienne asked her to write the play for her, bringing together Wersba's theater and writing experiences to form an association with a woman she had long admired. It also seems to be happening with her small-press publishing company, which draws upon Wersba's expertise as a writer and teacher together with her lifelong interest in book collecting. Wersba calls this phenomenon "synchronicity"—the coming together of one's inner and outer lives—those happy coincidences that somehow seem fated if one remains open to them.

There are other patterns in Wersba's life. For instance, she has always liked animals more than people. As a child, she mourned the loss of her cats more than the disintegration of her family when her parents divorced, and she housed stray dogs and cats in her college dorm room, her New York cold-water flat, and her New York country homes. In North Haven, she spends countless hours watching the wildlife in her own yard and in the nearby woods and marsh. She is fascinated by wild birds, particularly swans, that inhabit the wetlands extending from her backyard, and she photographs them regularly. And she is dismayed by the hunters who kill the deer living in the woods of North Haven, and speaks out against them publicly. Now that Zue is gone, their Norfolk terrier, Willie, has become Wersba's main companion.

But although she may prefer animals to people and describes herself as a loner, Barbara Wersba has formed a number of strong relationships with people throughout her life. Older people mentoring younger people is a recurring theme in Wersba's life. Connie Campbell, Eva Le Gallienne, and Charlotte Zolotow fulfilled this function for Wersba as did her agent Pat Schartle along with many teachers, theater directors, and college professors. In turn, Wersba has mentored many young writers through workshops, writing classes, and tutorial sessions. Some of Wersba's students publish their work, but most of her students are women who write as a means of self-discovery, as a way to make sense of their lives. Wersba understands this need because it is a motivational force in her own writing. She tells her students they must write from themselves, about feelings and experiences they have known firsthand. She cautions them not to write for style, that style will come from the depths of one's personality when the writing is honest. But she does want them to experiment with language and encourages them to write poetry, "even though they think they can't, because it's the essence of language" (Janeczko, 93).

In her own writing, Wersba, like many of her students, writes for self-examination, discovery, and understanding, but she also writes because fiction enables her to rearrange her life—to put the pieces together differently.[8] As she does this, she enjoys exploring various literary forms within children's and young adult literature and the challenge that shorter literary works demand. She chooses to write for young people partially because she feels this portion of her past is an enigma to her and writing from a young person's point of view helps her to better understand the past, sometimes even come to terms with it. She writes for young people because she still understands the loneliness, the fears, the uncertainties, and the frustrations they experience, and she wants to hold up hope. As she once put it, "we are all frogs who hold within us the beauty of the prince. The only surprising thing is that we do not know it."[9] She also writes for the pleasure of recognition when someone appreciates her books (Janeczko, 94).

Wersba's most moving experience as a writer came when she was volunteering at a rummage sale to raise funds for the local animal shelter. Like other writers in the community, Wersba donated from her own library, including copies of books she had written herself. A woman came to the table where Wersba was working, picked up *Let Me Fall Before I Fly,* and mentioned that she already had a copy and that of all the books in her library, it was her favorite. When Wersba told her she had written the book, the woman burst into tears and Wersba did as well. The woman gave Wersba a big hug and thanked her for writing a book that was so important to her. Although Wersba never saw the woman again, the spontaneity of the situation and the sincerity of the woman's emotions were enough to make Wersba say, "If this is the most moving thing that happens to me in my career as a writer, it is enough, because I really reached one person."

Because her writing is so completely personal, so autobiographical, and because she writes for herself first, Wersba is pleased and grateful to have as many readers as she does. Although her young adult books are popular with sensitive teens, they are also read by an enormous number of adult readers in this country. Wersba is surprised to have such a large older readership, people in their 20s and 30s, people who are not teenagers, but young adults in the true sense. Perhaps this crossover readership appreciates that Wersba understands the child, the adult, the child within the adult, and the eternal struggles between children and their parents.

Wersba is also fascinated by the tremendous popularity of her books in foreign countries. They have been translated into German, Danish, Swedish, Spanish, and Japanese. Her foreign sales are actually better than her U.S. sales, and she is quite popular in England. "Perhaps," speculates Julie Fallowfield, Wersba's agent, "compassion that has the universal appeal to transcend nationality is one reason Wersba's books sell so well abroad."[10] In addition, Wersba's fan mail indicates that teens from other countries read beyond their immediate experiences more readily than do American teens. Reviews from British publications frequently mention Wersba's wry humor. Whatever the reasons, Wersba is very happy to know the books are going out into the world, into areas she herself will never venture.

Barbara Wersba seems to have been right in her intuition that she had what it takes to be a writer. Still a loner—she's shy, even reclusive—Wersba thrives on long hours of quiet work alone in her studio. The imagination that helped her endure the loneliness of childhood, her introspective nature, her intelligence, her sensitivity, and her sense of humor all intertwine as she weaves stories that speak to countless readers. Her experiences as an adolescent in New York City, a successful actress, a lover of animals, and a caring friend, coupled with her curiosity about the world around her translate into intriguing stories for young readers. And finally, her determination, her belief that there is a synchronicity to life, and her willingness to take risks have all worked together to help her accomplish any goal she sets for herself.

When she wrote *The Dream Watcher,* Wersba entered on the crest of the genre that was to become young adult literature. Since then she has written 15 more young adult novels, almost all of which tell the story of a "younger person who needs to be mirrored, who is neglected at home and needs one older person to say 'You are very special, and I think you will go far.' " Just as *"The Dream Watcher* touched a cord with many people," so have her subsequent novels. Wersba's early works were groundbreaking, dealing with such tough issues as alcoholism, marital stress, drugs, premarital sex, strained parent/child relationships, pacifism, sexual orientation, unlikely friendships between people, and June–December romances. She continues to explore these topics in her later books as well as introduce others such as AIDS and homelessness. The gender of her characters, their artistic dreams, their sociological situations, and the time periods in which they live change, but, says Wersba, "I think I've only written one story, and many writers only write one story. My story is based on the fact that I didn't get what I needed from my parents. So I had a lot of teachers and mentors and good adults who made my life quite wonderful. That's the most important thing, and that's the story I tell in my books."

But Wersba's is not a simple story, and because it has endured, in its various manifestations, throughout the genre's growth and development, it has touched several generations of young adult readers. Clearly, Barbara Wersba has made a significant contribution to the field of young adult literature; both Wersba herself and her novels have done much to shape this relatively new field.

Robert Wersba (Barbara's father—center) with his wife, Josephine (Barbara's mother—right), and his mother, Eda (Barbara's paternal grandmother—left), in the late 1920s. *Courtesy of Barbara Wersba*

Barbara as an infant at the Belmont Hotel in Chicago, Illinois, in 1932. *Courtesy of Barbara Wersba*

Barbara as a five-year-old in 1937.
Courtesy of Barbara Wersba

Barbara and her cousin Lois in San Mateo, California, in the early 1940s.
Courtesy of Barbara Wersba

Barbara, age 11, in *Listen Professor* in Burlingame, California, in 1943. *Courtesy of Barbara Wersba*

Jo Wersba (Barbara's mother—right) and her mother, Susan Farmer Hampton (Barbara's maternal grandmother, known as "Mama Susie"— left), in San Francisco in 1945. *Courtesy of Barbara Wersba*

Barbara at 16 in her mother's apartment in New York City about 1948. *Courtesy of Barbara Wersba*

Barbara rehearsing Shakespeare at Bard College in 1954. *Courtesy of Barbara Wersba*

Barbara standing with her father on graduation day at Bard College in 1954. *Courtesy of Barbara Wersba*

Wersba as Marguerite Gautier in *Camino Real,* by Tennessee Williams, at Princeton University in 1954. *Courtesy of Barbara Wersba*

Above: Wersba with her acting teacher, Paul Mann, in New York City in the late 1950s. *Courtesy of Barbara Wersba*

Left: Eva Le Gallienne in the first production of *The Dream Watcher,* performed in Westport, Connecticut, in 1975. *Courtesy of Barbara Wersba*

Wersba with Eva Le Gallienne and director Brian Murray at a rehearsal for *The Dream Watcher* at the Seattle Repertory in 1977. *Courtesy of Barbara Wersba*

The Palisades Country Store. *Courtesy of Barbara Wersba*

Zue Sharkey in her office at the United Nations in the late 1960s. *Courtesy of Barbara Wersba*

Wersba in Sag Harbor in 1984. *Courtesy of Barbara Wersba*

2. Finding Oneself: *The Dream Watcher; Run Softly, Go Fast;* and *The Country of the Heart*

The Dream Watcher

I'd better begin this story by telling you that until a month ago I was quite a mess.[1]

Thus begins *The Dream Watcher,* Barbara Wersba's first young adult novel. This is the story that came to Wersba in a voice so urgent she set aside the historical novel she was writing to take a tremendous literary leap into the world of 14-year-old Albert Scully and his unconventional relationship with 80-year-old Mrs. Orpha Woodfin. As Albert Scully describes how Mrs. Orpha Woodfin changed his life by helping him discover who he is, he introduces character types, themes, motifs, places, situations, emotional underpinnings, and stylistic characteristics that reappear in various forms throughout Wersba's subsequent young adult novels. His story, an important one for a variety of reasons, deserves detailed attention.

Albert Scully is the quintessential miserable teenager. He feels like a total failure, and his soul, that which he believes to be the best part of himself, is trapped and troubled. His interests are curious for a boy his age, setting him apart from others. For instance, he likes to garden, collect recipes, watch foreign plays on Channel 13, visit the Natural History Museum in New York

City, read novels in the local library, and paste literary quotations on the wall over his desk. He enjoys writers like Shakespeare, Thomas Wolfe, Walt Whitman, Sherwood Anderson, and Thoreau—and reads them instead of doing his homework—but he has no one to talk to about them. In fact, he does not have anyone he can talk to about anything. Fortunately, his cat, Orson Bean, does comfort and amuse him.

Albert's mother is a dissatisfied housewife who "walks around being a movie star in her mind" (15). She longs for a life of gracious luxury, but has to settle for unreliable electric conveniences. Albert's father, whom Albert likens to Willie Loman in *Death of a Salesman,* is an ineffective insurance salesman who once dreamed of being an airplane pilot but is now enslaved by installment payments for appliances that break before the final bill arrives. Albert's mother nags Albert about everything from his low high-school grades to his lack of friends to his reading interests. His father sometimes weakly defends Albert but generally takes passive refuge in alcohol. The sadness he feels for his father adds to Albert's general state of depression. The unhappy Scully family lives in Blythewoode, a suburban housing development in New Jersey.

Mrs. Orpha Woodfin, the 80-year-old neighborhood eccentric, lives a few blocks from Albert in a dilapidated old house she refused to sell to the developers. Just when Albert thinks he is about to go insane, he meets this unique woman. Although he has not had a real conversation with anyone for five years, Albert is able to discuss literature with Mrs. Woodfin and disclose his feelings about himself. He tells her, over a glass of sherry, that he has been feeling suicidal and blames himself for his "lousy" life. As he puts it, "I'm lousy in school and don't fit in anywhere and have all these peculiar tastes that embarrass my mother" (30–31). Mrs. Woodfin angrily responds: "All you are saying is that you are different! A quality which puts you in the company of saints and geniuses" (31). These are welcome words to Albert, who sees being different as his major problem in life.

Albert has been depressed because he doesn't feel a part of what his peers, parents, and society in general seem to want out of life. He sees through the sexual bravado of the other boys. He can't fit into the "go to college, be a success, make lots of money" view of life. He once visited Greenwich Village to see if he could relate to the hippie crowd, but found he could not. Feeling lost because he can't connect with any group, Albert asks, "What else is there?" Mrs. Woodfin replies with her characteristic formality, "What else, sir? Why, yourself. Have you ever thought of just being yourself?" (71). Albert hadn't thought of this and doesn't really understand what she means. After Mrs. Woodfin recites Thoreau's passage about hearing a different drummer, Albert finally understands. He should just be himself, even if it means being viewed as a failure. That's what Thoreau did, and that's what Mrs. Woodfin has done. Albert finds himself through these "very happy dropouts" (74).

Mrs. Woodfin tells Albert that she grew up in a titled British family. When she was 16, her one ambition was to become a great actress. She worked hard and her talent was recognized world-wide. She had many triumphs as an actress, but she gave up all the fame and glory when she was in her 20s, because she realized she had achieved everything but happiness. She moved to America, suffered financially from the stock-market crash, and bought a country home in New Jersey. Now she just lives simply and enjoys nature. She's a lot like Thoreau, who gave up financial security in the pencil-making business for the simplicity of Walden Pond.

Albert and Mrs. Woodfin become close friends. While Albert sips tea, she sips sherry, and they nibble sandwiches and talk about past experiences, war, pollution, materialism, the educational system, conformity, and their private dreams. Mrs. Woodfin reassures Albert that feeling different is not a bad thing and supports his peculiar tastes; she compliments him on his looks and his intellect. Albert believes her and his self-concept improves as he begins to see himself through Mrs. Woodfin's eyes. She encourages him to follow his dreams, to march to a different drummer, but also warns him he must meet conventional obligations, such as graduating from high school, in order to earn the right to be unconventional. She tells him this in the hospital shortly before she dies, and she reiterates her belief that he will be all right.

When she dies, Albert is distraught to learn that Mrs. Woodfin fabricated her past. She was never an actress. She came to the States in 1938 to teach at the Crowley School but was fired for drinking. An American relative had given her the old house, and she lived on welfare. His mother tells him this almost triumphantly because she wants to make him face the truth. His father finally succeeds in stopping her, saying that she has "nagged him until he doesn't know who he is anymore" (165). He even puts his arms around Albert, a gesture Albert had longed for but to which he cannot respond. Later, alone in a vacant lot, Albert balances the painful discovery that a person he loved could deceive him, by realizing that despite the lies, Mrs. Woodfin had given him something—a belief that he would become somebody. In spite of everything, Albert has discovered who he is, and he is going to be all right. His soul, no longer ailing, has been released.

So who exactly is Albert Scully? Albert is a loner, a boy different from his peers and most of society, who rarely connects with other people. He is the son of parents who do not understand him and are unable to nourish his soul. Living in a vague, foggy world, Albert lacks self-knowledge and misses helpful clues like the drummer passage in *Walden*, a book he has read several times. But when he does connect with a kindred spirit, he begins to gain self-awareness. Talking with Mrs. Woodfin helps him to realize he has long admired people who are individuals, but he is just starting to make the connection between individuality and his own identity. He also starts to discover his opinions about world issues through his wide-ranging discussions with Mrs. Woodfin.

Albert is not an angry young man placing blame on others for his feelings of loneliness, nor does he lash out in frustration. Instead, he turns his anger and frustration inward and, blaming himself for his "lousy" life, feels depressed, even suicidal. He has compassionate thoughts about others, but hides his feelings. For example, he feels sorry for his father, who has resigned himself to a mediocre job and a demanding, unappreciative wife. Although he feels the awkwardness when his mother humiliates his father in front of him, Albert does not try to console him. Like his father, he is undemonstrative, and he feels guilty for this. When Albert does act on his compassionate feelings, it often turns out badly. For example, he proposes to a pregnant girl in his eighth-grade class, even though he really doesn't like her, because he admires her for not telling who the father is. But as a result, he is rejected by her, ridiculed by his mother, and later insulted by the girl's sister. He is also perceptive about others' motivation and behavior; he understands his mother's vision of herself as a movie star, but knowing she would never want to discuss this, keeps his thoughts to himself. Sensitive, introspective, tense, and lonely, Albert desperately needs a friend, and it is understandable that he is drawn to the gracious, extroverted Mrs. Woodfin.

Like Albert, Mrs. Woodfin also needs a friend. Always attired in the same tattered ankle-length black-velvet dress she says she wore in *Hedda Gabler,* speaking in a formal, rather grand style with an English accent, and living amidst cheerful squalor, she is indeed eccentric. Her knowledge of both literature and the lives of writers is extensive, and she frequently quotes literary passages. Broad-minded about everything except the Vietnam War and conformity, she is eternally optimistic, sees the positive in every situation, and believes human beings are basically good. Albert likes her because she laughs like a child when she is amused, gets directly to the heart of the matter when he has a problem, and listens to him carefully and respectfully.

In many ways, Mrs. Woodfin is the opposite of Albert's mother, who complains about everything, is obsessed with cleanliness, and pretends not to hear him when she dislikes what he says. Albert considers this selective listening an interesting survival technique, commenting that "you could write a whole book on it" (128)—which is essentially what Barbara Wersba did. Albert's mother affects him more deeply than he knows, and his friendship with Mrs. Woodfin helps counter her debilitating influence.

Albert's father drinks to cope with his demanding, unsatisfied wife. He also uses humor as a defense. For example, when Mrs. Scully talks about modernizing the kitchen by getting a "Cooking Island," he asks, "How do you get to it—by boat? (95). Albert appreciates his father's humor; his mother does not. Albert, though not an outwardly humorous person himself, has a darkly comic way of envisioning situations. For example, during the "Cooking Island" conversation, he thinks:

> And I had this vision of him making payments on Cooking Islands for the rest of his life. Then one day he would die, and since he didn't have any friends there would be no one to come to the funeral but me and my mother and all our appliances. I could just see the TV set and the vacuum cleaner and the washing machine sitting in the funeral parlor trying to cry, but unable to because they didn't have feelings. (95)

This "Cooking Island" represents Mrs. Scully's adjusted dream in life. If she cannot have the glamour depicted in old movies, she wants a home straight out of *House Beautiful* magazine. She also wants Albert to get good grades, go to college, and be financially successful. Mrs. Scully does not need a Mrs. Woodfin to encourage her to pursue her goals, because her dreams already dominate the household. As a young man, Mr. Scully dreamed of becoming an airplane pilot. But his future wife guided him toward a job as an insurance salesman, thinking he would get promoted to the executive level, which he never has. Now he pays the bill for his wife's movie/magazine-inspired dreams.

Mrs. Scully spends a lot of time and energy badgering Albert about his grades, but his vision for himself does not include further education and financial success. He essentially rejects the American dream and longs to sail tugboats on the Hudson River and gaze at the New York City skyline or move to environmentally unspoiled New Zealand. The conflict between Mrs. Scully and Albert over who will decide, and direct, his dream is an important one in a novel entitled *The Dream Watcher*. Albert is certainly in a position to observe how dreams or daydreams affect the lives of several adults, and in turn these observations influence his decisions about holding on to his own dreams.

The use of deception raises significant questions in *The Dream Watcher*. There are many lies told within the story, forming a pattern of deception that is both positive and negative, instructive and destructive. Throughout the novel Albert is no stranger to deception. He clearly perceives the school psychologist's insincerity, with his overly familiar approach and "hip" communication style. Albert dismisses him as a phony and a liar, realizing that he hates deceptive adults who "pretend that they are on your side, when all they were doing was giving you the axe" (81). But Albert responds to the psychologist in kind, telling him what he wants to hear—that he "digs" him. He even attempts to take his advice, but it doesn't work.

Perhaps Albert sees through this collegiate-type professional masquerading as a "cool" friend, because Albert himself is prone to deception. He confesses to having been a "terrible liar" since he was a child, inventing maladies and parental occupations to impress, or perhaps momentarily hold the attention of gullible questioners. And when his mother forbids him to see Mrs. Woodfin, he creates a string of extracurricular activities to cover the truth that he is visiting her. These lies are useful because they allow him a life and a soul-saving relationship, but they deepen the gulf between him and his parents. His mother eagerly accepts his active new life, as Albert knew she would, because it's what she wants to hear.

But Mrs. Scully also wants to hear that Albert's grades are improving, and he can't deceive her about this. While she is lecturing him about all the sacrifices she has made so he can have a better life than she has, Albert realizes—"Zap! Pow! Wham!"— that she had actually been doing all this for herself as an investment in him, and she is angry because her expensive stock is not paying off. He longs to clear up all the lies, for them to "be honest with each other and maybe love each other again" (129), but it doesn't happen.

Albert may be perceptive about his own and other people's lies, but he never suspects Mrs. Woodfin would deceive him. Indeed, he believes "Mrs. Woodfin would have burned at the stake rather than tell a lie" (112). He trusts her completely, accepting her opinions of him as truth. So of course he is devastated to learn that she has deceived him about her life. She was ordinary—"just an alcoholic who told lies" (169). He can't understand why somebody he loved would trick him; they were friends and she did not need to impress him. He had been uncharacteristically honest with her, not feeling any need to lie to impress her. But as he contemplates the situation, he sees that she was lonely and needed friends. She had not lied to him about the importance of being oneself or her beliefs in what is good and beautiful. Actually, he realizes, she *had* been special because she had given him the gift of himself.

When Albert's mother insists he know the truth about Mrs. Woodfin, his father wants to know, "[w]hat's so important about the truth?" (165). It's an excellent question. Mrs. Woodfin had lied, but the effect of her deception was positive both for Albert and herself. She had not deceived him the way the school psychologist had when he feigned concern. On the contrary, she gave him her genuine attention and respect. And he had responded with unaffected love and admiration. In many ways, Mrs. Woodfin really was an actress. Her life had become a grand act, and the last role she played was crucial to the soul of a lonely teenage misfit.

Perhaps there is a parallel between Orpha Woodfin's story and the theater itself: members of an audience are often moved, even transformed by a performance that appears real, while the actors themselves are nothing like the characters they play. Indeed, many of them, as Wersba knows now but did not as a child, are alcoholics just like Mrs. Woodfin. Nevertheless, the effect of the actors and the play and the staging and all that goes into a production can still be enormously powerful and convey truths to those who watch. Albert finds himself despite Mrs. Woodfin's compulsive drinking and lying, just as Barbara Wersba gained determination from the first professional play she saw, even though Laurette Taylor, as Wersba learned later, had to be sobered up by Eloise Armen before playing Amanda Wingfield in *The Glass Menagerie*. Appearance can create reality.

Wersba uses the friendship between Albert and Mrs. Woodfin to show that unconventional/improbable relationships can change one's life for the better. Closely tied to this theme is the motif of parental disapproval of one's friends and an older mentor. Mrs. Woodfin is not the first of Albert's friends Mrs. Scully has disapproved of. When Albert was 10, he had a close friend named Billy Marks. Billy's impoverished family always treated Albert with love. But the one time Billy came to Albert's home, Mrs. Scully treated him as though he were uncouth. Billy got the message, and the boys' friendship cooled. Mrs. Scully initially disapproves of Mrs. Woodfin, calling her the crazy old lady who gave her son alcohol. When Mrs. Woodfin becomes ill and Mrs. Scully learns of her supposedly noble birth, Mrs. Scully allows Albert to visit her. (She is, however, resentful that Albert pays more attention to this old woman than he does to his parents.) But upon learning that Mrs. Woodfin is a fraud, Mrs. Scully returns to her original uncharitable opinion of Albert's 80-year-old friend. Because Mrs. Scully hears only what she wants to hear and because Albert can't talk to her, she is oblivious to the benefit that Albert has derived from his relationship with the unconventional Mrs. Woodfin.

Another important aspect of *The Dream Watcher* is its numerous literary references, connections, and quotations. Albert mentions Shakespeare in the first paragraph and, a few pages later, compares his father to Willy Loman from *Death of a Salesman*. He reads serious authors and poets like Thoreau, Thomas Wolfe, Walt Whitman, and Edgar Lee Masters. Mrs. Woodfin's house is filled with great literary works from which she quotes frequently throughout the story. The passages she recites or Albert reads to express an emotion or emphasize a point not only show the importance of literature to Albert and Mrs. Woodfin but also enrich and elevate the story as a whole.

A former English teacher, Mrs. Woodfin clearly values great literature as a comfortable intellectual companion. Albert thrives on discussing his interpretations of plays like *King Lear* with Mrs. Woodfin. As narrator, he exerts several literary opinions of his own: James Jones, Harold Robbins, and John O'Hara are popular with teens because they are dirty but read like literature (9); Hemingway is masculine to the point of making a guy who reads him feel inferior (10); books about youth improving itself, like *To Kill a Mockingbird,* are boring (78); and *The Valley of the Dolls* is poorly written (75). He reads the books Mrs. Woodfin loans him, ponders passages she suggests, and often looks to literature, whether in written or visual form, for help in making sense of his confusing world.

Literature does play a role in helping Albert come to terms with himself, but, as he states from the beginning, he attributes his newfound sense of self to his relationship with Mrs. Woodfin. From the outset of *The Dream Watcher*, it is clear that Albert will be all right. This book is a personal account, so obviously Albert does not commit suicide, and he speaks of his problems in the past tense, so this is clearly the story of how he got better. What saves this book from being a typical how-youth-improves-itself story is the engaging voice of Albert Scully. Albert sprinkles his narrative with his thoughts, reflections, and revelations. He is unaware of the self-deprecation and wry wit that characterize his worldview. Wersba speaks through this lonely, unwittingly humorous adolescent to comment on social ills, other writers, and even her own work. The story's upbeat ending provides hope for those who identify with the once-miserable Albert. And because this story is biographical, which "means you have to be honest" (110), Albert comes across as a trustworthy narrator. His story incorporates many truths about the pain of adolescence; it rings true.

Albert's story rings true because it is emotionally grounded in Wersba's experiences as a teenage loner who had difficult relationships with both of her parents and looked to other older people for mentoring. She weaves her extensive literary background and experience in the theater into both the plot and the characterization. *The Dream Watcher* is Wersba's first attempt to explore her own adolescence through a literary lens, and as she believes she has primarily one story to tell,[2] many aspects of this book recur in subsequent works and are easily recognized characteristics of Wersba's unique style of writing for young adults.

The Dream Watcher established Wersba as an important voice for teenage readers. Like *The Pigman*, it came out in 1968, the year after *The Outsiders, The Contender*, and *Mr. and Mrs. BoJo Jones*[3] heralded the beginning of a new genre of literature written specifically for teens. This was not traditional romance or adven-

ture, but literature, called "the new realism," that deals straight-
forwardly with teenage problems. *The Dream Watcher* was generally well received. Zena Sutherland of the *Saturday Review of Literature* dubbed it "an unusual and perceptive book;"[4] Pamela
Bragg of *Publishers Weekly* said it was "a humorous and sensitive
portrait of two unforgettable characters;"[5] and Virginia Haviland
of *Horn Book* noted that "the frankness, the realism, the close-
ness to adolescent idiom give the telling an important conviction,
creating a picture all too true."[6] John Weston in the *New York
Times Book Review* said the book could be reassuring to teens like
Albert who worry about being different and stated that "*The
Dream Watcher* is loaded with adult wisdom, but Miss Wersba
weaves it smoothly into her over-all creation." In addition Weston
said that "Miss Wersba has bravely undertaken the difficult stylistic accouterment of much quoted material from Shakespeare,
Shaw, Rilke, Thoreau, and Wilfred Owen to underscore her
points."[7]

Most critics welcomed the character of Albert Scully into the literary world. As Polly Goodwin of the *Washington Post*'s Book
World section put it, Wersba, "with skill and compassion, has created a good, honest human being, an individualist who needs his
dreams and will have the strength, you feel sure, to be himself.
She has written an unusual and very fine book about an extraordinary friendship, a book that is thoughtful, often funny and with
a hero to remember."[8]

Reviewers, however, had differing opinions about Mrs. Scully.
Sutherland appreciated how Albert tells his story candidly, giving
a searing picture of his ambitious, petty, nagging mother and a
pathetic one of his frustrated, henpecked father (Sutherland, 69).
Several years later in a *School Library Journal* article entitled
"The Skirts in Fiction about Boys: In a Maxi Mess," Diane Gersoni Stavn acknowledged that Wersba treats Mr. Scully sympathetically but criticized the author for having portrayed Mrs.
Scully as "a castrator who constantly puts down her unsuccessful
hard-drinking insurance man of a husband. . . . but [Wersba]
shows little patience with the wife's own frustrations."[9] Also concerned with images of women in young adult fiction, Maggie

Parish entitled her *English Journal* column "The Mother as Witch, Fairy Godmother, Survivor, or Victim in Contemporary Realistic Fiction for Young Adults." Over 10 years after *The Dream Watcher* was published, Parish used Mrs. Scully as an example of a mother who is shown primarily as a witch or destructive influence on her son or daughter. Mrs. Scully, says Parish, is "stereotyped but the book works as literature anyway; the protagonist's redemption is an absorbing theme, and while we never see the positive attributes that his mother may have, we do see, and the protagonist must confront and accept, the negative attributes of his 'fairy godmother' [Mrs. Woodfin], who is a whole person with strengths and weaknesses after all."[10]

The positive intergenerational relationship between Albert and Mrs. Woodfin brought *The Dream Watcher* immediate praise. Sutherland wrote: "In this odd and touching companionship between an adolescent boy and an eccentric and engaging old woman, there is a singular charm; they complement and comfort each other" (Sutherland, 69). Twelve years later, in an article entitled "A Positive Image of the Elderly in Literature for Children," Jerry J. Watson called *The Dream Watcher* a "timeless and superbly crafted story" and used Mrs. Woodfin as an example of an elderly eccentric, "someone not willing to conform to society's expectations," who "challenges the reader to accept differences in all people."[11] Of course it was the character of Mrs. Woodfin and her relationship to Albert that attracted Eva Le Gallienne to *The Dream Watcher* and led to Wersba's writing the script for its stage production.

Critics were quick to recognize the similarities between *The Dream Watcher* and *The Catcher in the Rye*. The reviewer in *Time* magazine saw Albert Scully "as a mini-Holden Caufield [who] is as real as he can be."[12] Similarly, Laura Polla Scanlon in *Commonweal* wrote: "Readers will be reminded of *The Catcher in the Rye*. The theme is similar and the same bitter-sweet humor runs through it. But this is no imitation. It's an eloquent restatement of the old plea for the individual."[13] The critics and Eva Le Gallienne were not the only ones who recognized the importance of Wersba's first novel. Wersba also received an enormous amount of mail from readers of *The Dream Watcher*. Thinking about it now she says:

> That book seemed to reach out to more people than most of my books. I guess it must be the common experience of young people and very old people bonding together. I received letters from old people; I received letters from kids. At the time, 1968, that young adult first-person voice had not been used as much as it is now. So the voice of *The Dream Watcher* was attractive to people. All of these early first-person voices came out of *Catcher in the Rye,* including mine, although I didn't know it because I wasn't conscious of it.

The idea for the character of Mrs. Woodfin occurred to Wersba at a party she attended in Snedens Landing. Wersba was taken to tea at the home of a famous character in the neighborhood, Marion Gray. Mrs. Gray lived in a run-down house, was enormously fat and crippled, and was the world's greatest expert on lace. Wersba was enchanted by this brilliant, eccentric old lady who lived in squalor but could see only beauty and told wonderful stories. It was spring and the sides of the road were teeming with wildflowers and Mrs. Gray said, "Look at them marching up and down the road like little kings and queens." Wersba considered Mrs. Gray a poet and was very moved by her. That brief encounter and the voice of a lonely teenage boy who felt misunderstood caused Wersba to write *The Dream Watcher*.

Run Softly, Go Fast

In *Run Softly, Go Fast* Wersba writes of another misfit who experiences difficulty with his parents and gains support outside of his immediate family that eventually enables him to find himself. Although this novel includes some of the same themes, topics, and other characteristics found in *The Dream Watcher,* Wersba introduces other aspects that intensify the story she tells in her second young adult novel, which is set in New York City in the late '60s.

Run Softly, Go Fast is David Marks's written attempt to explain and understand his feelings about his father, Leo Marks. Following Leo's death, 19-year-old David begins a journal in which he describes the way his childhood feelings of love and admiration for his father changed to disgust and hatred as he grew up and learned more about what kind of man Leo really was. This 200-page journal, David's "whole life in a notebook,"[14] is an in-depth journey toward self-discovery in which he analyzes the roles various people play along the way. He addresses each of these people directly at times and at other times just writes his memories, trying to make sense of his life. As he tells his story, his voice is filled with anger and confusion, leaving little room for humor, just caustic wit, as when he describes Leo as "a Jew who swallowed the Protestant Ethic and died of it" (8). As David writes, he hopes for enlightenment and forces himself to confront painful, sometimes submerged memories as he struggles with his feelings about what it has meant to be Leo's son.

Leo Marks, the son of Jewish immigrants, grew up in abject poverty and wants a better life for his son. Taking advantage of his boss's financial difficulties, he becomes a partner in a Seventh Avenue clothing business and eventually takes over the whole company. He moves his wife and son from their shabby 73rd Street flat to a plush apartment on Riverside Drive, where they live an affluent lifestyle. Leo wants his son to emulate him, but David daydreams. Leo encourages him to be athletic, but David prefers to paint pictures and write poetry. Leo urges him to attend a prestigious college and become a financial success, but David refuses to go to college. Leo wishes David would make influential friends, but David spends his time with Rick, whose character and sexual orientation Leo questions. He advises him to marry a nice, gentile girl, but David moves in with a college dropout. Leo demands that his son look presentable, but David has long hair and wears sandals. Leo insists his son visit him as he lies dying in the hospital, but when David finally comes, they fight. Leo needs his son's approval, but feels David is ashamed of him. Leo wants his son, but he loses him. In many ways, Leo's desires for David resemble those Mrs. Scully has for Albert in *The Dream Watcher:* Leo wants his son to carry on the American dream, which his own father failed to achieve but which he himself has succeeded in realizing. What Leo fails to realize is that David is also a self-made success—but he's an artist, not a businessman.

David Marks, like Albert Scully, has parents—his father in particular—who don't understand him. And like Albert, David is socially alienated. At first his isolation disturbs him, and he tries to please the other boys in order to be popular at school, but then he realizes that he does not need them, because his art is what matters to him. Both boys believe that they represent unsuccessful financial investments. But whereas Albert is self-deprecating and blames himself for his miserable life, David is angry and directly blames his father. David pinpoints Leo's crude personal habits, his corrupt business practices, and his extramarital affairs as factors contributing to his disillusionment with Leo and his subsequent confusion about life. But it is Leo's treatment of David's friend Rick that drives David to leave home at the age of 17. David desperately wants to disassociate himself from a father who is so cruel as to call his best friend a "lousy little queer" (174). David believes that Leo's vicious words eventually cause Rick to give up the process of becoming a conscientious objector and, for the sake of proving his manhood, succumb to family pressure to join the military.

David wants his father to understand and respect him. He writes him a long letter explaining how he feels about his life and their relationship and asking for his support, but Leo never acknowledges the letter. David wants him to meet and like his girlfriend, Maggie, but Leo works late the night they come for dinner. David hopes his father will attend his art show, but Leo doesn't appear. David wishes his father were proud of him as an artist, but when Leo indicates he is, David doesn't hear him. David rejects him—his crudeness, his insensitivity, and his cruelty—all that he himself does not want to become.

David and Leo Marks are locked in a bitter love/hate relationship. Both are equally proud and stubborn, and neither wants to relent. Leo can't let go of his dreams for David; David fears that if he acquiesces even a little, he will lose the self for which he has sacrificed so much to find. The conflicts and issues of control in *Run Softly, Go Fast* are similar to those between Albert and his

mother in *The Dream Watcher*. There are also similarities
between the two boys. For example, David, like Albert, perceives
at times what his father wants or needs from him but does not
give it, and the wall between father and son thickens until it is
impossible to permeate. David also looks to others for what his
parent is unable to offer.

Leo's brother, Benjamin, is the first person to whom David
turns as his admiration for his father fades. Benjamin, an aes-
thete, a scholar who works in the Jewish Library, takes him into
the world of Judaism and scholarship. He encourages David's
interest in the arts, accompanying him to museums, encouraging
him to write poetry, and buying him art supplies. But most
important, Benjamin loves David as he is; he does not try to fit
him into a mold. Leo, of course, is jealous of this brother, demean-
ing him as a "dreamer who spends his lifetime writing a book!"
(45). But David loves, admires, and trusts his uncle. He turns to
him when he learns Leo is having an affair with a fashion
designer, a devastating discovery. But Benjamin, not wanting his
serene world disrupted by this knowledge, tells David he is overly
critical of Leo and must have imagined something that isn't true.
Like Mrs. Scully, he chooses not to acknowledge the situation.
David and Benjamin are never close after that.

Disappointed by his uncle, David turns inward and studies Zen,
Rilke, and the artist Tchelitchew. Intrigued by Tchelitchew's
style, David imitates him, but adds his own poetry to the painting. Then in his senior year he meets Richard Heaton, a new student at his prep school, and David's life changes. Rick is a fellow
painter whose parents don't understand him either. The two of
them quickly develop an ardent friendship, with Rick taking an
advisory role. He introduces David to poets, novelists, essayists,
and philosophers who open a whole new world to him. They visit
art museums, browse in bookstores, listen to records, and carry
on involved discussions. Rick talks openly about being a pacifist
and his plans to apply for conscientious objector status if he is
drafted into the Vietnam War. He encourages David to disagree
with Leo and take charge of his own life. Rick shares his poetry
and his paintings with David, but David wants to wait to share

his own work until he creates something he really likes. Rick won't be put off, however, and David finally shows him his paintings. Immediately recognizing that David has talent but has been imitating Tchelitchew, Rick tells David to develop his own style. When Rick suggests David paint not what he sees, but who he is, David instantly comprehends the truth in Rick's criticism, and he writes, "[S]o I found myself. Not the whole self, but a seed" (77).

David's painting flourishes, his admiration for Rick grows, their friendship intensifies, and Leo, who earlier encouraged David to make friends, doesn't like it. Like Mrs. Scully, he resents his son's becoming close to someone else. Leo begins to insinuate that there is something wrong with Rick and, concerned about his sexual orientation, eventually throws him out of the house after catching Rick and David roughhousing. (174). Even though David leaves home because of Leo's behavior, he is profoundly embarrassed by the incident, and his friendship with Rick is strained. But later when Rick tells David that his C.O. (conscientious objector) application has been denied and he will join the army rather than embarrass his family by going to jail, David feels betrayed, even more than he did when Ben refused to acknowledge Leo's infidelity. He never sees Rick again. When David leaves home at the age of 17, he moves in with Marty, his friend since childhood, who has an apartment in the East Village and attends NYU. In addition to providing David with a place to live while he continues to attend prep school, Marty, who turns out to be a moonlighting hippie and the local drug dealer, offers to supply him with drugs and girls. The night David learns of Rick's betrayal, he accepts Marty's offer and they go to Cowboy's place, where David drops acid. Now David spends most of his time with his new "family"— Cowboy, Happytime, Valiant, Preacher, Tiny, and her son, Dormouse. Several months later when David learns Rick has been killed in Vietnam, he completely falls apart. Wracked with guilt and remorse, he becomes heavily involved with drugs until he meets Maggie Carroll.

Maggie, as David puts it, brings him home (148). He says this in the context of their sexual relationship, because he had heretofore been unable to make love. But Maggie's comforting, undemanding manner enables him to be close to her. Of course Maggie literally brings him home because he moves in with her, but she brings David home in other ways as well. Maggie brings David back to his art, understanding the importance his work holds for him and helping him arrange and put on a one-man art show. She helps him find more of himself and confirm who he is. And she tries, albeit unsuccessfully, to help him resolve his conflicts with his father, because she senses this is important for David, even if he will not acknowledge it. But when David takes Maggie home to meet his parents, Leo is not there. Leo's refusal to meet Maggie is ironic because he would have liked her had he allowed himself to like anyone with whom David was close. Maggie, a gentile, is kind, gentle, and educated—just the qualities Leo himself had sought in a wife. But to Leo, the lack of a marriage license or at least an engagement ring automatically makes her a "tramp" (162).

Maggie is, in fact, a bit of a mother figure for David. She is a year older than he is, more sexually experienced, and the kind of nurturing person who adopts stray dogs and abhors cruelty and injustice. When he first tells her he hates his father, she says, "Never mind. We'll be each other's parents" (11). But later when David in an angry moment tells her to "stop being my mother," she replies, "I don't want to be your mother. You insist on it" (168). David's words are interesting because his own mother does not try to control his life in the way he accuses Maggie of doing—his father does. His mother just submits to her husband.

David's mother, Dolly, loves and supports Leo up to the moment he dies. She understands his hunger for financial success, his deep love for David, and his insatiable need for his son's approval. Because she was happy taking care of her family when they were poor and lived on 73rd Street, the move to Riverside Drive is difficult for her. But Dolly adjusts; she starts looking chic and doing volunteer work like the other wives of successful businessmen. She knows about Leo's shady business dealings and his extramarital affairs, but she forgives him. She periodically asks David to try to understand his father, to show a little compassion for him, but David cannot. In his father's final days, she orders David to visit Leo in the hospital.

But David and his father do not reconcile before Leo's death, and David, after three months of writing his journal, is left to realize he only knows his own side of the story and that there probably was more good in Leo than he was willing to acknowledge. As the pages in his notebook run out, he forces himself to recall some words Leo spoke during their last encounter. Leo had read the reviews of David's art show and was proud of him. But David had blocked these words out, probably because they did not fit with the image he had created of his father. In addition, David had not told his father that he remembered the happy times they had together before their conflicts began, and now he realizes it is too late. This failed communication motif runs throughout *Run Softly, Go Fast* just as it did in *The Dream Watcher*. In both novels, people—Mrs. Scully, Benjamin, David—hear what they want to hear and are unable to say what needs to be said. Thus generation after generation of parents and children continue to hurt each other, and yet somehow they survive. As David begins to understand this pattern, he manages to make peace with his memory of his father and, in this way, finds another part of himself.

The use of deception and the search for truth, topics addressed in *The Dream Watcher,* also figure in *Run Softly, Go Fast.* Much of David's anger toward his father centers on the lies Leo tells in the course of his everyday life. He keeps two sets of books for his business, carrying on the same dishonest business practices he once criticized the former owner for; he deceives his family by being unfaithful to his wife; and he lies to his business associates about David, saying he has been accepted at Dartmouth and will be entering the business world, marrying a nice girl, moving to the suburbs. But the lies go both ways. As David examines his life, he remembers lying as a child about his father, saying he was a doctor who operated on people; then as a young teenager, saying Leo was in the publishing business. And after Leo forbids him to see Rick and tells him to have Marty get him some dates, David thinks: "I will capitulate the better to deceive you" (81). He invites Marty, Marty's friends, even girls over, as a camouflage, and sees Rick on the sly. Nonetheless, honesty is important to

David, and he is disillusioned not only by Leo's lies, but also by Benjamin's inability to see Leo for what he is and by Rick's relinquishment of his adult-self to his parents. Because they are unable to live up to his expectations, David perceives them both as dishonest.

David also distrusts memories, saying: "Memory lies, smooths over the rough parts" (12). He wants to get past the smoothed-over parts to find the truth. Mr. Scully once asks, "What's so important about the truth?" David initially believes the truth will set him free, but in the end, he understands that "there are only fragments of truth, little lights in the darkness" (204). It is impossible to know the truth of anyone, even oneself, because the truth keeps changing as one grows and sees things differently. This, David learns, is the nature of truth. And because the truth is amorphous, one can't ever be certain one is right. There is always room for error; there is always cause for reconsideration; there is always the possibility of forgiveness; and there must always be respect for humanness. So David comes to trust memories because "maybe one person can never know another . . . just memories" (204). Drained of his anger and hatred, David is no longer obsessed with finding the "truth." He is able to let his memories of his father rest in peace.

Truth and deception are abstract concepts Wersba explores in both her first young adult novels, but she also addresses some concrete issues, such as the Vietnam War, the hippie scene, and conflicts over money. None of the characters in either book seems to agree with the war, but in *Run Softly,* Rick's thoughts, his report on the disillusionment of his army mates, and his death represent much stronger statements against the war than do the opinions expressed by Albert and Mrs. Woodfin. Both Albert and David come to reject the hard-core hippie scene, but David does so after living in it for eight months, whereas Albert only experiences life in the streets of Greenwich Village for a day or so. The conflicts over money differ even more markedly. In *The Dream Watcher,* money is at the center of the problems between Albert's parents: Mrs. Scully wants more than her husband can financially provide. In *Run Softly, Go Fast,* Leo Marks tries to impress others with his financial success and use his money to control his son. Dolly Marks does not seem to care if she is wealthy or not, but thinks mainly of Leo's happiness. As Rick points out, and David doesn't hear, Leo tries to give David money and material objects because that is all he thinks he has to give. Misunderstandings about money, its importance and its meaning, however, cause substantial conflicts in both families.

In addition, both books contain many literary references. However, whereas references in *The Dream Watcher* are mainly to classic writers like Shakespeare, Rilke, and Thoreau, literary references in *Run Softly* include more contemporary authors and poets such as Neruda, Hesse, and Camus. Popular singer/poets like Leonard Cohen and Joni Mitchell are also mentioned in *Run Softly*. But in both stories, characters have literary discussions, loaning books is an important part of friendly relationships, and Wersba's literary background is obvious.

Religion and sexuality are two major topics that figure more prominently in *Run Softly* than they do in *The Dream Watcher*. *Run Softly* is tightly situated in the Jewish culture. Leo Marks's father left Poland because of religious persecution; his brother, Benjamin, is devoutly religious and teaches David that the importance of being Jewish is that the Jews have survived. Leo, however, wants to assimilate, and David criticizes Leo because he is ashamed of his heritage. Yiddish words punctuate the text and Leo speaks with recognizable Jewish phrasing and cadences. Other spiritual/philosophical elements also exist, as when David studies some Zen and existential philosophy. Although a religious/spiritual element does at times enter into the discussions Albert has with Mrs. Woodfin in *Dream Watcher,* religious issues are much more pronounced in *Run Softly*.

Sex figures in *The Dream Watcher* mainly to show how Albert differs from the other boys his age who brag about nonexistent sexual exploits. Sexuality, however, is a major aspect of *Run Softly, Go Fast*. Masturbation, impotence, premarital sex, extramarital sex, and homosexuality are all of great importance to David and the integrity of the story. The age difference between Albert and David may be one reason for the way Wersba chooses to treat the topic of sexuality in each novel, but the two years between these books' publication may also be another. Sexual realism was new in literature for adolescents when *Dream Watcher* first came out. Up to this time, premarital sex might occur before a story commenced as in Ann Head's *Mr. and Mrs. BoJo Jones* (1967), but that book focused on the aftermath: the young couple's difficult adjustment to marriage and to the death of their child. By 1970 the topic of teenage sex had been introduced in numerous novels for teens, but sexual orientation was still a taboo subject, so Leo's accusations and David's pondering what "if the words were true" (174) broached uncharted territory. Of course any treatment of sexuality at all was quite controversial, but Wersba does not write of these topics for sensational reasons, but rather because they are issues which enter into many teens' lives and profoundly affect their relationships with their parents.

Stylistically, *Run Softly* is quite complex. An ongoing journal, it is written in stream-of-consciousness style. David starts to delve into memories, backs off, and later revisits them as he forces himself to relate *everything* that took place, no matter how painful it is to remember. So although the story he recounts does have a forward movement, and David is a different person at the end of the book than he was at the beginning, the narrative style is recursive, not linear. Wersba skillfully intertwines narrative, associations, questions, and reflections, providing not only information about what happened between David and Leo, but also a strong emotional sense of the situation David is confronting. She also subtly imparts wisdom via David such as: "Love is color-blind and sex-blind and age-blind. Has to be, or it makes no sense" (174–75). Humor is scarce within David's mind, and the wit that surfaces is usually dark. For example, at his father's funeral he amuses himself by thinking about the finite amount of burial ground and asking: "What will happen when all the land is used up? Will they shoot the dead into orbit? Celestial cemeteries: Grief on the launching pad? (OK, Smithers, let's begin the countdown for the funeral. Ten, nine, eight, seven, six . . .)" (18). This funeral musing is reminiscent of Albert Scully's appliances-at-his-father's-funeral-parlor daydream, which is simultaneously funny, compassionate, sad, and characteristic of the bittersweet tone in *Dream Watcher*. The tone for much of *Run Softly* is just plain bitter until David works through his resentment toward his father. But as in *Dream Watcher*, Wersba shows the progression of the protagonist's thoughts, giving his voice an authentic ring.

The authenticity in David's voice was praised by most critics but questioned by a few. When reviewing *Run Softly* for the *Horn Book*, Sheryl B. Andrews considered it a mistake to lump this book with the many others written about "alienated youth, the drug scene, and Middle Class America," because in spite of its preoccupation with these often tritely treated topics, this book "rings true" and "succeeds in clearly and forcefully conveying basic human weakness and blindness as well as the universal need for love and understanding, which must begin with the individual himself."[15] Writing for the London *American Observer*, Nancy Garden declared *Run Softly* a "true book" because it is based on true emotions.[16] John Rowe Townsend, however, wrote in the *New York Times Book Review* that Wersba just threw in "chapters on hippie life, drugs, sex and the rest" because these were "currently fashionable" topics for teens and the positive ending seemed forced and didn't "quite ring true."[17]

While some critics had difficulty with the novel's ending, others heralded it as one of the book's major strengths. In an article for the *School Library Journal* entitled "The Critical Myth: Realistic YA Novels," Roger Sutton criticized young adult problem novels for typically dealing with only one issue and providing easy solutions and happy endings, but he offered *Run Softly* as an example of a realistic novel with a provocative ending that shows that sometimes life's problems remain unsolved. Sutton credited *Run Softly* for its inability to be categorized as a "death book" and because it is descriptive of David's growth toward self-acceptance and reliance rather than prescriptive about how to deal with problem parents.[18]

Several sources recognized *Run Softly, Go Fast* as one of the year's best books. The *New York Times* placed it among nine teenage-fiction titles heralded as outstanding books of 1970.[19]

The American Library Association (ALA) selected it as one of 1970's Best Books for Young Adults.[20] The committee chose 34 books that year. In addition, Kenneth L. Donelson and Alleen Pace Nilsen list it in *Literature for Today's Young Adults* as one of three titles selected for their prestigious Honor Sampling for the 1970 publication year. The other two books were Maya Angelou's *I Know Why the Caged Bird Sings* (Random House) and *Bless the Beasts and Children,* by Glendon Swarthout (Doubleday).[21] *Run Softly, Go Fast* was also honored outside the United States when it received the German Juvenile Book Prize in 1973, an award that carried a $15,000 prize.

Run Softly has continued to be recognized as an outstanding book. In 1986, Ken Donelson compiled a list he titled "Fifty YA Books Out of the Past Still Worth Reading; or, Enjoyment Is There *If* You Search for It." The first 23 books come from a period spanning nearly 100 years, from 1868 (Louisa May Alcott's *Little Women*) to 1966 (Scott O'Dell's *The King's Fifth*). The last 27 come from the "new realism" period, which consists of the years from 1967 through 1974. Donelson listed *Run Softly, Go Fast* as one of these last 27, calling it "Wersba's best novel."[22] In 1993, the American Library Association culled its yearly Best Books for Young Adults lists and selected the top 100 books published for young adults in the previous 25 years (1967–1992). This list, announced in 1994 and called the "Best of the Best," includes *Run Softly, Go Fast.*[23]

Well-received when first published and periodically recognized as a noteworthy young adult novel, *Run Softly, Go Fast* is, nevertheless, out of print. Educators have lamented this fact, and when the Assembly on Literature for Adolescents of the National Council of Teachers of English (ALAN) surveyed, in 1991, its past presidents, asking them to identify out-of-print YA books that they would like to see back in print, *Run Softly, Go Fast* was one of the 17 titles receiving enough votes to be included on the ALAN Encore List.[24] An equally instructive sample was printed in the Booksearch column of the National Council of Teachers of English's (NCTE's) *English Journal.* Readers responded to this question: What work that is now out of print deserves to be reissued? Educators were not limited to YA titles, and the suggestions included professional resources, autobiographies, biographies, short-story collections, and novels. *Run Softly, Go Fast* was the only young adult novel recommended, and Angela Leone, the high-school teacher who had used it successfully for 10 years and wanted it reissued, wrote she suspected it was out of print because publishers might consider it dated. She notes that the book's time-less theme and the current renewed interest in the '60s make this an excellent time to consider reissuing *Run Softly, Go Fast.*[25]

As in the case of *The Dream Watcher, Run Softly* draws its emo-tional base from Wersba's own experiences. She was always at odds with both her parents, even as an adult, and truly under-stands unresolved parent/child conflicts. This is Wersba's most autobiographical novel in terms of the Jewish side of her family. The character of Leo is a combination of her own father, Robert, and her uncle, Louis, two very conservative Jewish men who were strictly raised by a tyrannical father who eventually committed suicide. Leo reflects many of the attitudes the Wersba brothers had toward bringing up a child. Barbara and her cousin Lois were treated much the same way as David. Both her father, when she lived with him in California and when she visited him after the divorce, and her uncle, with whose family she spent a lot of time, had a heavy-handed, old-fashioned, authoritarian attitude toward Barbara and Lois. Uncle Louis was trying to raise Lois and Bar-bara as he was raised. Like Leo, he was in the garment business, but unlike Leo he was a cultured man.

There is a lot of the Jewish side of Wersba's family in the father's attitude in *Run Softly*. Both Barbara's father and uncle wanted to assimilate. Because they had grown up in the early part of the twentieth century, they were sensitive about being Jewish. Much of the sadness in the hospital scene is drawn from Wersba's feelings when her own father was dying in Los Angeles. The par-ticular events in the book are not real, but Leo's emotions are very close to Barbara's father's. Everything in fiction, Wersba reminds us, gets translated into other terms.

The hippie portion of *Run Softly* is based on Wersba's firsthand observations of some of her younger friends in Greenwich Village.

Although she never used drugs herself, she did sit in on LSD sessions in the '60s. She watched as her friends took acid and listened as they talked about their experiences. She saw many people out of control in those days and used these experiences to capture the reality of the hippie culture.

Stylistically, Wersba did things she liked in this book, such as going back to an idea and expanding upon it. She found it interesting to do this because it provided a new challenge. She was pleased to discover she could handle a complex narrative style effectively. *Run Softly* is clearly more stylistically complicated than *The Dream Watcher*. It is also more intense because although both protagonists are serious and highly introspective, anger tends to lend itself to passionate writing more readily than does depression. In addition, the content of *The Dream Watcher* is much more innocent, and the general mood of *Run Softly,* drawn as it is from the drug culture of the '60s, is more electrically charged. *Run Softly, Go Fast* is Wersba's most intense as well as most complex novel. Perhaps this is why many consider it her best.

The Country of the Heart

The Country of the Heart is the story of 18-year-old Steven Harper, who attends the local community college in Cromwell, New York. Steven, an aspiring but misunderstood poet, has a passionate, albeit brief, love affair with the famous American poet Hadley Norman, who is 40 and, although Steven doesn't know it, dying from cancer. In her own alternating harsh and gentle manner, Hadley teaches Steven about poetry and about love, about life and about death. Five years after her death, Steven writes to Hadley, describing his feelings, both then and now, about her and the gifts they gave each other.

The story line in *The Country of the Heart* is similar to Wersba's first two young adult novels: a lonely teenager whose parents don't understand him is mentored by someone outside the family who helps him find himself. It differs in that Steven's family remains in the background, mentioned only minimally to show the contrast between them and Hadley Norman. Steven's parents are straightlaced. They don't drink and they expect him to help out around the house. His mother, a minister's daughter with "small-town ways," devotes much of her time to the church, believes in the "concept of family," and always says "everything will be fine."[26] His "grossly masculine" father (11), who sacrificed a life of adventure to support his family by running a small business, is disappointed in both his children, with whom he quarrels bitterly. He detests Steven's interest in poetry, his books, and his moodiness, wanting him to be like other kids, rather than the "freak" he perceives him to be. Looking back, Steven sees his family as "two children and two adults: afraid to love one another, living our lives in unspoken despair" (10). Five years later, his father is paralyzed from a stroke; his rebellious younger sister, the only family member he could relate to, has run off; his mother no longer smiles; and Steven has gained enough perspective to understand them a little better.

But as an 18-year-old misunderstood by his parents, lonely and even suicidal, Steven sustains himself with poetry. He began writing poetry when he was 12, but he has not been published. Steven reads and memorizes the poetry of Rilke, Pound, Joyce, Eliot, and Yeats and longs to write as beautifully as they do, aching because he fears his words will never equal theirs and his life will come to nothing. Like David Marks in *Run Softly, Go Fast,* Steven has artistic aspirations his family neither understands nor supports. He has no one with whom he can discuss the poetry of others, his own poems, or his dreams of becoming a famous poet. Hadley Norman's poetry has long provided him solace, and he is carrying a worn copy of her *Three Landscapes* when he learns she has moved into a carriage house in his neighborhood. Even before he musters the courage to knock on her door and ask for an autograph, her mere existence comforts him, somehow making him feel he may survive the distress of his lonely world.

Hadley Norman is not at all "a goddess, a legend, a myth" as Steven imagined she would be (10). Answering the door in an old plaid bathrobe and slippers, her gray-streaked blond hair disheveled, she is visibly irritated about being disturbed. Their first meeting lacks anything close to the immediate rapport David Marks felt with Rick or Maggie, or that Albert Scully soon felt with Orpha Woodfin. In fact, except for her drinking and disorderly house, Hadley Norman seems the exact opposite of Mrs. Woodfin. Her solitude is self-sought; her fame is real; she is cruel, self-centered, ungracious; her dog is more important to her than any person; and she initially resists helping a fellow human being in distress. But of course her circumstances are very different. Dying of cancer, Hadley is suffering from pain. She also suffers the curse of being a talented poet: she is compelled to write poetry, even when it brings her no pleasure. Steven feels spiritually close to Hadley even before he meets her, so it is understandable that he falls in love with her, even though she is not what he expected. Familiar with schoolboy crushes, Hadley tries to discourage Steven with ridicule, but they eventually become lovers. She softens during this period of their relationship, and Steven becomes less critical of her gin-drinking and pill-swallowing. But as her condition worsens, Hadley again pushes Steven away. They fight constantly, and Hadley harshly tells Steven it's over. He sees her only once more, in the hospital a few weeks before she dies. This time she tells him she really had loved him, and then asks him not to return.

Steven did not know Hadley was ill, and his grief is mingled with rage when he learns her situation and understands that she tried to protect him by not telling him the truth. Here, as in *Dream Watcher* and *Run Softly*, the issue of deception emerges. Like Albert and David, Steven has lied to his parents in order to spend time in a relationship they would not approve of. Steven, therefore, is not above deception, but he is still saddened to learn he himself was deceived by someone he loved. Hadley's reasons for deceiving Steven are both selfish and noble. She is, as her former husband, John Norman, later tells Steven, a very private person. But Steven seems correct when he interprets her deception as a desire to protect him, to enable him to take the precious gift of her time—a gift he might not have taken had he known she was dying. Hadley's deception seemed necessary, but as soon as she starts lying about doctor appointments and saying she has anemia rather than telling Steven the truth, their relationship begins to deteriorate. They argue continually until a wall "like stone" rises between them (94).

Closely tied to the topic of deception is the question of whether one person can really know another. When Steven encounters John Norman in Hadley's vacated house, John does not believe Steven has been Hadley's lover. He says he knows "Hadley rather well," but Steven tells him he doesn't know her at all. Of course Steven doesn't know Hadley at all, either. Intimate as they were, he did not know she was dying. Nor did he know she was still involved with her ex-husband, John, or what she was like as a child, or what her life as a celebrity had been like, or who her previous lovers had been. He may have known her daily habits, but he did not know and never would know all the people who had "shaped and shattered" her life (114). He had been fascinated by the complexity of her personality, but in the end he realizes his knowledge of her is incomplete. Similarly, Albert never really knew Mrs. Woodfin, and David never really knew Rick or his father. All three characters are left with bits of knowledge, numerous questions, and many memories about people who are now dead. Perhaps this is all that can be expected because as Hadley Norman put it, "Nobody knows anybody very well" (63).

Another theme common to Wersba's first three novels is that love, whether it be between friends or lovers, transcends social conventions. As David realizes in *Run Softly,* real love must be blind to color, sex, and age. Albert's friendship with Mrs. Woodfin was not restricted by their age difference. Likewise, the discrepancy between their ages does not prevent Steven and Hadley from forming a physical relationship. Steven describes their attraction as two needs coming together: Hadley's "need for life and strength" and his own "need for all the worlds [he] had never known" (65). Steven realizes he is in love with Hadley much sooner than she does, and she is reluctant to reciprocate his feelings and become sexually involved with him. She says people will find out, and he says he doesn't care. Actually, neither does she. The concept of a teenage boy having his first sexual experience with an older woman is not new to the world of literature, but it

was unheard of in young adult literature when Wersba wrote
Country of the Heart. Unconventional liaisons are important in
Wersba's works, not for their shock effect, but because they show
the importance of and need for human connections.

The importance of dreams, a theme also found in all three novels, underlies *Country of the Heart,* although the word "dream" is
never actually mentioned in this context. Steven has dreamed of
becoming a poet since he was 12 years old. Like David, Steven
knows what his dream is, he just has to discover how to achieve it.
His father represents failed dreams, and Hadley represents
achieved dreams, so naturally he is drawn to her and will risk
almost anything for her advice. As Steven's reluctant mentor,
Hadley immediately recognizes that his poems imitate Rilke and
tells him his writing must come from his own feelings and experiences. Her message resembles Mrs. Woodfin's suggestion to
Albert to be himself and Rick's advice to David to create rather
than imitate. And like both these other mentors, Hadley gives her
student a key to himself: he can find himself through his art, and
once he finds himself, his poetry will improve. She has clearly
pointed him in the right direction.

Although the basic story line and several themes are echoes
from Wersba's first two novels, the protagonist and the style of
Country of the Heart make it distinctly different. Steven Harper
reveals his story through a letter he writes to Hadley five years
after her death. He writes to say, "I never told you how I felt,
never once spoke of the depth of my love for you, love made fool-
ish by being young." By writing to tell Hadley "how it was in
those days" and to find her again "in the country of the heart"
(3), he makes the reader privy to the soul-felt account of his passion. The words he chooses befit an emerging poet, weaving
images and emotions with narrative and analysis.

The first of Steven's poems that Hadley finds genuine is a love
poem written about her called "Song." It is an extension of what
Hadley has taught him, reflecting the inner self he has kept
silent. Steven's song is filled with anguish, admiration, desire,
elation, anger, hatred, and despair. He is much too earnest for

humor, but Wersba pokes fun at herself via Steven when Hadley calls him a "Holden Caulfield writing poetry" (60) and chides him with "Oh, Steven, you're using your *Salinger* voice again" (56). Imagery abounds in Steven's love song: Hadley is "a candle blowing in the wind. . . . a face in the sea" (10). Lyrical phrases flow as Steven pens the feelings he has had during their lovemaking: "Hadley, all the mountaintops are shining with the thin gold of dawn and all the deserts are streaked with purple pools, shadows. All the seas rise up, frozen and green, whipped with foam, because we are together" (84). This self-indulgent, adolescent writing style is apropos for Steven because his manner of writing dovetails with his impetuous, undisciplined sexual desire and need for love. Once again, Wersba has got the voice just right.

Most critics responded favorably to *The Country of the Heart.* Reviewers like Mary Silva Cosgrave, in the *Horn Book,* saw the story's sensitivity, noting that the affair between Steven and Hadley could have become maudlin but instead becomes a moving relationship.[27] As with her first two novels, the voice of the narrator drew comment. Georgess McHargue, in the *New York Times Book Review,* considered it a "perceptive look at 'growing up literary' in which the voice of the narrator and the character of Steven are unmistakably one, alternatively naive, self-conscious, pretentious, and yes, talented."[28] The American Library Association named it one of the Best Books for Young Adults, 1975. *The Country of the Heart* was made into the television movie *Matters of the Heart* in 1990 and starred Jane Seymour.

According to Wersba, the character of Hadley Norman is a composite of several people she has known, but she had Eva Le Gallienne most strongly in mind when she created certain aspects of Hadley's character. Wersba wrote *Country of the Heart* during the beginning of her friendship with the temperamental Le Gallienne. Le Gallienne read the book, but never knew Hadley had been partially modeled after her. Other parts of the book came out of Wersba's personal relationships, including her friendship with noted theater director Margaret (Peggy) Webster, who was dying of cancer. In Wersba's words:

As I was writing this book I was watching someone carry on with her work to the very last minute. She was writing her autobiography until the moment she died. She was also a fine actress and she gave her own farewell performance in a town hall on Martha's Vineyard, even though she was in terrible pain. Peggy Webster was tough and angry and valiant and brave—and a lot of that quality came into the character of Hadley.

Thinking about the book now, Wersba says *Country of the Heart* embarrasses her: "Now the book seems almost overwrought. It seems overly emotional and I can't read it. At the time it seemed all right, but now it seems too naked and exposed." On the other hand, she loves the film made from this book because the producer, Martin Tahse, was faithful to the book in ways "that are unheard of in Hollywood." Wersba admired Tahse's adaptation tremendously and still talks with him on the phone.

Each of Wersba's first three novels is emotionally intense in a manner fitting its protagonist's attempt to find himself, and readers still respond to the intensity of these struggles. Things changed a bit for Wersba after she wrote these books, and her next novels take on quite different tones.

3. Accepting Oneself: *Tunes for a Small Harmonica, The Carnival in My Mind,* and *Crazy Vanilla*

The protagonists in Wersba's next three novels are unconventional teens from affluent families, whose parents show them little positive attention. These characters suffer low self-esteem or question their identity, but each of them finds a friend or has an experience that generates self-acceptance and precipitates a step through adolescence toward adulthood. Although despair is common among these characters, their degree of teenage angst is much less intense than earlier Wersba protagonists David Marks, Steven Harper, or even Albert Scully experienced. Increased humor tends to lighten the tone of these novels, although the emotions, situations, relationships, and issues involved are often similar to those in Wersba's first three novels.

Tunes for a Small Harmonica

In *Tunes for a Small Harmonica* 16-year-old Jacqueline Frances McAllister falls in love with Harold Murth, her 30-year-old poetry teacher at Miss Howlett's School for Girls, one of New York City's finest prep schools. A rebel who once tried to abolish the school's uniform requirement, J. F., as she prefers to be called, decided at age 12 to dress like a boy for the rest of her life. At 16, she lives on

Park Avenue but looks like a "teenage cab driver"[1] or, as she says, a transvestite. She once worried she was gay but now knows she is heterosexual. J. F. was initially bored by Harold Murth's lectures on obscure poets, but when he recites a poem by Charlotte Mew, he becomes transfigured, and J. F. instantly falls in love with him.

Harold Murth is no longer just a pale, pedantic young man; he is saintlike in his golden, ethereal beauty, and she must know everything about him. Her investigations lead her to believe he is poverty stricken and unable to finish his Ph.D. thesis on Christopher Smart because he cannot travel to Cambridge, England, to complete his research. J. F. plays her harmonica on street corners and passes the hat in New York City's theater district to raise the money necessary for his travel. She is financially successful until her parents discover what she is doing and forbid it. Believing she and Harold belong together because "he is the yin of [her] yang" (53), J. F. decides they must marry. But first she intends to seduce him so that their relationship can become more comfortable.

So deep is her love for Harold and so desperate is her desire to attract him that, along with reading all the obscure poets she can, J. F. doffs her boy's clothing and pays him a surprise Christmas Eve visit dressed in female attire. In the course of their awkward conversation, Harold mentions that his wife, from whom he is temporarily separated, will be coming to visit him on Christmas. Shocked and devastated to discover that Harold is married and thinks of her only as a "very dear child" (163), J. F. also learns that Harold himself comes from an affluent family but chooses to live "Spartanly, in the manner of a scholar" (161). She realizes he is oblivious to her feelings for him and the meaning of her gifts, including the check for $1,000 that he will not accept. Needless to say, seduction is now out of the question.

Utterly depressed on Christmas morning, J. F. decides to commit suicide by jumping, weighted down by her Webster's Unabridged Dictionary, into the East River. But before leaving, she opens the Christmas present from her best friend, Marylou Brown. The chord-playing harmonica Marylou has selected moves

J. F. greatly and makes her regret that she did not receive it until the "day of her demise" (166). At that moment Marylou calls and says that Melvin Babb, whom J. F. met at a play-reading, was so impressed with J. F.'s appearance he might offer her a part in a film. J. F. skips her suicide, and that afternoon Melvin describes to her the part of Spunky, a teenage tomboy who is a front for two con-artists. Noticing J. F.'s harmonica in her pocket, he quickly decides Spunky should also play the harmonica.

In a sudden stroke of clarity, J. F. understands that Melvin is "a fat phony [who] was going to take me and my Tappan Zee High School outfit and my harmonica and make a fast buck out of them" (172). Melvin liked her not for herself, as she had thought, but because she was a "freak" he hoped to exploit. Deciding she really is odd, J. F. realizes she likes herself the way she is *because* she doesn't look or sound or act like anyone but herself. She has spent her whole life "worrying about being a peculiar person, when that was what [she] was *meant* to be in the first place" (173). Finally accepting herself for who she is, J. F. walks out on Melvin. Having come to terms with a troublesome aspect of her self, J. F. can now play her harmonica for herself and the peace it brings her.

Peacefulness is a welcome feeling because throughout her experience with Harold Murth, J. F. fluctuates between the depths of despair and the heights of hope. For example, on the day before Christmas vacation, she wakes up feeling depressed and suicidal because Harold has been aloof. Then she recovers an envelope he discards and sees he has doodled her name all over it. Considering this a clear sign of his love, she is instantly elated. Although her story is definitely an unusual one, the emotional swings of adolescence J. F. experiences are common.

Unfortunately, J. F. does not have a set of concerned parents to help her through her troubled teenage years. Her father, Mr. McAllister, is an executive for Standard Oil who spends little time with his wife and even less time with his daughter. J. F. sees so little of him that when she was a child she thought he frequently traveled to a place called Conference and proudly told her friends her important father was once again in Conference. As an adolescent her rare encounters with him are generally fraught with embarrassment.

Overly concerned with physical appearance, J. F.'s mother, Mrs. McAllister, is not only unable to lend her daughter emotional support, but strongly contributes to her feelings of inadequacy. The wife of a successful businessman, Mrs. McAllister divides her time between beauty parlors and department stores. She is generally quite composed, but J. F.'s dressing like a boy and marching in a Gay Lib parade distresses her greatly. She finds her daughter's androgynous appearance humiliating, and tells her so. J. F. responds to these ego-deflating "discussions" by tuning her mother out. As she puts it, "It was incredible how quickly my mother could make me feel like a cipher" (42). The two of them have nothing in common except that they are ashamed of each other.

The irony of the situation is that J. F. really does have concerns about her sexual identity and could benefit from talking with a concerned adult. But instead, she is left to her own resources. Thinking she must be gay, she reads up on homosexuality at the public library, but books such as *Homosexuality and Low Blood Sugar* are not very helpful. She begs her best friend, Marylou, to kiss her but is disappointed with their experiment in passion. She is seeking camaraderie when she marches in a Gay Lib parade, but feels no connection with the other demonstrators. J. F. wants to be gay because this would help her understand why she prefers to be eccentric. It would explain her preference for male clothing and her pleasure in carrying a Swiss Army knife. It would help her understand why she feels "so sexually unawakened [she is] almost a neuter" (114).

Mrs. McAllister sends J. F. to a psychiatrist, but Dr. Waingloss's ineptitude and J. F.'s creative evasion tactics render their sessions useless. These sessions do, however, provide Wersba with opportunities to broach the topic of sexual orientation and raise questions about the Freudian theory of homosexuality. When J. F. asks him why people are gay, Dr. Waingloss replies, "The cause of homosexuality is a rejecting father and an overly intimate mother" (86). J. F. internally questions this simplistic answer, wondering "what about gay orphans? Or people raised on an Israeli Kibbutz? Or what about gay Arabs—gay natives in darkest Africa? All of them couldn't have had a rejecting father and an overly intimate mother. What about gay sheep and gay cows? Dr. Waingloss you are a fraud" (86). Rather than help with her sexual confusion, all Dr. Waingloss does is make J. F. further mistrust him as a therapist.

One reason J. F. mistrusts Dr. Waingloss is that he is an eclectic therapist and, therefore, has the great convenience of not being required to make sense or be committed to one approach. He can plagiarize at will from existentialist, Freudian, Jungian, transactional analysis, or interpersonal psychological theories. He has a penchant for free association, which J. F. tries to evade by telling him bogus dreams—such as the one about the giant harmonica that she encountered on the streets of New York, wearing a business suit and carrying a black umbrella. She also mentally removes herself from his lectures by daydreaming about traveling with Harold.

Just as J. F. reads to understand homosexuality, she reads to defend herself against Dr. Waingloss. She reads Freudian casebooks as well as popular psychological theories espoused in books such as *You and Your Gestalt; Death—the Ultimate Transaction;* and *Interpersonal Madness.* When J. F. finally decides to trust Dr. Waingloss and open up to him, she finds him distraught because his analyst of 10 years is moving to Chicago. In a classic role reversal, the man who always spurned her personal questions breaks down and confides in his 16-year-old patient. J. F. realizes she must rely upon herself to achieve the answers she seeks. Although Dr. Waingloss does not help J. F. directly, the relationship between these two characters enables Wersba to poke fun at psychology and therapists, as well as include some very funny scenes in the novel.

Passages dealing with J. F.'s character flaws are also quite humorous. J. F. is impulsive. A week before she falls in love with Harold, she is browsing in Abercrombie and Fitch, her favorite sporting-goods store, when she notices a store detective following her. Angry because she assumes he is judging her on her appearance—her "Down with Reality" sweatshirt, faded Levi's, and old sneakers—she quickly gives the clerk her mother's charge card and instructs him to "charge and send" a small canoe. The detective blushes when she tells him she is taking it to her fishing lodge in Canada. That little canoe caper costs J. F. her allowance for quite some time and renders her financially strapped when she decides to send Harold to England.

Financial need brings out another character defect: J. F.'s ability to engage in deceptive behavior. Wanting to know all she can about Harold, J. F. follows her uncontrollable impulse to invade others' privacy and looks at his file in the school office. She also lies to her mother when she takes off for her busking gigs, and of course she deceives the theater crowd with the sign that says she is a music student. In addition, she forges notes from her mother so she can skip school when Harold is ill with the flu, and she tells her mother she likes Dr. Waingloss in order to make Mrs. McAllister believe she is getting her money's worth. J. F. is well intentioned but dishonest.

J. F.'s best friend, Marylou, on the other hand, is a paragon of virtue. With her limp bangs, crooked smile, and bitten fingernails, Marylou is a compassionate and loyal friend. Concerned about J. F.'s chain-smoking, Marylou buys J. F. her first harmonica and thereby inadvertently provides the means for J. F. to earn Harold's travel money. Although she is reluctant to do anything immoral and counsels J. F. on the difference between love and a crush, she assists J. F. in her efforts to help Harold financially and even to seduce him. J. F. appreciates her greatly and understands the look Marylou gives her that says, "I love you, J. F., but you need a keeper" (142). In many ways Marylou takes the nurturing maternal role J. F.'s mother is incapable of playing. Actually, Marylou has had much practice playing this part because she has been parenting her own irresponsible parents for years.

Marylou's parents, Samuel and Bradley Brown, are playwrights who earn their bread and butter writing the soap opera *The Secret Holocaust,* for which they solicit even J. F.'s suggestions for the plot. Mr. Brown once wrote a play called *Death of a Dentist,* in which "the dentist is a drug addict, and his wife keeps telling everyone that attention should be paid to him. In the end he commits suicide by taking an overdose of novocaine" (17). Bradley Brown's latest play is about a mechanical shovel that terrorizes small towns because no one is willing to stand up to its intimidation. Wersba does not mention *Death of a Salesman* or Hitler but the references are clear, making the parodies amusing. The presence of the Browns enables Wersba to have fun with playwrights, of which she herself is one. In addition, the plot in *Tunes for a Small Harmonica* reads like a soap opera, so Wersba is also making fun of herself in the process. Her jabs at directors and her commentary on the theater, via Melvin Babb, are a bit more caustic.

J. F. McAllister as narrator speaks directly to the reader, providing a first-person account that pieces together the story of Harold Murth. Unaware of the humor in her thoughts and actions, J. F.'s voice is innocent yet self-critical. In some ways J. F.'s voice reminds one of Albert Scully's in *The Dream Watcher,* although it occasionally, as when J. F. speaks to the memory of Dr. Waingloss, echoes the resentment expressed by David Marks in *Run Softly.* But it never reaches the fevered pitch of Steven in *Country of the Heart.* In many ways it is the voice of a mollified Holden Caulfield, pointing out phonies and punctuating with "goddamns," but using a lighter touch that indicates all will end well. J. F. McAllister is the first female narrator in Wersba's novels, but like J. F.'s appearance, her voice is androgynous.

The character of J. F. is based on a person Wersba knew when she was living in Rockland County. Wersba remembers this 30-year-old tomboy, who eventually became one of her writing students, as a wonderful grown-up kid. J. F. has many of her endearing qualities. J. F.'s harmonica-playing came from Wersba's own experience with a small harmonica that someone bought her as a birthday joke the summer before she wrote *Tunes.* Finding she could achieve quick success on the instrument, Wersba played it passionately for several months and passed the talent on to J. F. The character of Harold Murth grew out of one of Wersba's teachers in prep school—a pale, shy, aesthetic young man who taught history, not poetry. Wersba had a friendship very much like the one between Marylou and J. F. When she was in prep school, she had a best friend named Barby. They were together all the time, always at each other's homes doing homework, even though they attended different schools. They would meet every day at three o'clock halfway across town for hot chocolate. They had their first dates with boys together and remain best friends to this day. Wersba is now godmother to Barby's grown children.[2]

Reviewers praised Wersba's humor and sensitivity in *Tunes*. Most found it thoroughly entertaining; some called it a laugh-out-loud read. It was an ALA Notable Children's Book of 1976; an ALA Best Book for Young Adults, 1976; a nominee for the 1977 National Book Award for Children's Literature; and the *New York Times Book Review* named it one of the Outstanding Books for Teenagers of 1976. Female teenage readers for G. Robert Carlsen's 1977 Books for Young Adults Poll responded favorably to *Tunes,* finding it to be "something humorous that could be a real-life situation."[3] The starred review for *Booklist* referred to it as "a seriocomic look at 'teenagehood' that could provoke thought as well as laughter."[4] In the *Bulletin of the Center for Children's Books,* Zena Sutherland calls the book "funny, frank, and sophisticated," with "memorable characters, brisk dialogue, and a yeasty style."[5]

The Carnival in My Mind

Harvey Beaumont, 14 years old and five feet tall, is so distressed about being short and looking 10 years old that he wants to kill himself. He is miserable at the elite Lawrence School for Boys because he has no friends and is constantly hazed by the other preppies. His home situation—a Fifth Avenue apartment in New York City where he lives with his mother, at least five Irish setters, and the domestic staff—is only slightly more congenial. Harvey's mother, the famous Muriel Beaumont, who used to breed and show Irish setters and is now the president and sole member of the Irish Setter Rescue League of America, pays more attention to her dogs than she does to Harvey. Harvey seldom sees his father, who is a retired banker 20 years older than Harvey's

mother and who resides in the family's country home in Mill
Ridge, Connecticut. But even when Harvey's father lived with
them in New York City, he was rarely at home. In fact, until Harvey was in kindergarten, he thought Holmes, the butler, was his
father. Holmes, who has been with the family since Harvey's
mother was a child, remains the only person who shows Harvey
consistent attention. He even takes a polite interest in Harvey's
desire to write short stories, the one activity at which Harvey
feels adequate.

Harvey appreciates Holmes's reserved affection for him, but
what he really wants is his mother's attention. He is "desperate
to be noticed. Admired. Appreciated. Loved."[6] But she has always
loved her dogs more than people, and she devotes her life to them.
His yearning for Muriel's love is fed by a vague memory: he was
three and attending a dog show with her and she was unexpectedly kind to him, which made him feel loved. Harvey longs to
have his mother consider him as important as an Irish setter.

One day while riding the Fifth Avenue bus, Harvey meets
Chandler Brown, an aspiring actress. Struck by her eccentric
beauty and flattered by her attention, he accepts her invitation to
drink champagne at the St. Regis Hotel. Harvey learns Chandler
has been declared an unfit mother for her three-year-old daughter. The child lives with her maternal grandparents in Michigan,
and Chandler misses her terribly. Confiding that he always has a
carnival going on in his head, which is "just about the only thing
that keeps [him] sane," Harvey is astonished that Chandler
understands that his carnival is the way he defends himself
against loneliness (19). They become friends, and Harvey is proud
to be associating with an actress who seems oblivious to the six-
year difference in their ages and one-foot difference in their
heights. Basking in Chandler's kindness and optimism about his
short-story writing, Harvey spends as much time as possible with
her. He enjoys accompanying her to acting auditions and on shopping sprees at New York's most expensive stores, but her tiny,
cockroach-infested flat in Greenwich Village dismays him.

One afternoon when he is particularly depressed, Harvey and
his mother have an argument. Declaring he can do nothing right,

Muriel is unimpressed when Harvey triumphantly shows her a copy of *Horrors Unlimited,* the first magazine to have accepted one of his stories; she says it's "utter trash" (99). When he hysterically talks about killing himself, Muriel demands that Harvey compose himself and apologize for being rude to her. While his mother and the household staff prepare for a dinner party in celebration of one of the dogs' birthdays, Harvey quietly packs a duffle bag and leaves home. He moves in with Chandler, who welcomes him as a roommate. They sleep together for mutual comfort, not sex, although Harvey allows others to assume their relationship is sexual. After the first night, Harvey tells Holmes he has moved, but that he plans to visit the Fifth Avenue apartment regularly. As he predicted, Muriel does not even realize Harvey is gone.

Harvey continues to attend school, but does not do well in any subject except composition. He spends much of his time making the rounds with Chandler as she tries to get acting roles. Although always unsuccessful, Chandler remains hopeful. Her optimism infects Harvey, who begins to see life from a less gloomy perspective and no longer contemplates suicide. However, money becomes a problem. He and Chandler have agreed to split the household expenses, but she never pays her share. Even Harvey's generous allowance cannot cover their living expenses, so he decides to ask his father for a loan. During his brief visit to Mill Ridge, Harvey and his father have the most intimate conversation they have ever had. Mr. Beaumont defends his wife when Harvey speaks critically of her, and Harvey learns that Muriel's parents, who did not love her, sent her to boarding school until she was old enough to marry. She has always turned to animals because she can rely upon their devotion. Mr. Beaumont suggests Harvey try loving his mother instead of criticizing her. But he also offers to set up a bank account for him to cover his new financial needs. Harvey leaves, resenting his father's absence from the apartment and wishing they could communicate better. He still longs for his parents' approval, especially his mother's.

That night Chandler reassures Harvey that his life will be all right. When he expresses his concern about being short and his overall feeling of inadequacy, she tells him height is unimportant;

he is good-looking, capable, and smart, and she believes he will someday be a famous writer. Each of her words is "a diamond flashing in the sun" for Harvey, and he promises Chandler he will try to believe in himself (155). Acknowledging the mutual appreciation in their friendship, they fall asleep in each other's arms.

Chandler eventually gets a part in a play, but she is a failure. Harvey sadly realizes that despite her optimism, she may not succeed as an actress. He also notices that the many men who regularly call her have not been phoning so often. Around this time his story "At Night You Can Hear Them Eating" is printed in *Horrors Unlimited.* He sends a copy to his father and continues to work on his writing. Then Tommy Vanderbout, Muriel's professional dog walker, sees Harvey with Chandler. Tommy knows Chandler quite well and informs Harvey that she is a call girl and an alcoholic. Even though he wants to disbelieve it, Harvey knows it is true. Although sickened by the information and hurt by her deception, Harvey still loves Chandler and does not want to confront her with the truth. Chandler eventually approaches the topic of her shortcomings the night she takes him to his first real carnival and tells him she has decided to leave New York. She plans to return to Michigan and marry a respectable man who is eager to adopt her child. Harvey knows he will never see her after she leaves, but understands his relationship with her has changed his life.

Chandler has helped Harvey gain insight into himself, his family, and the nature of parent/child relationships. His relationship with Chandler temporarily filled his need for maternal love just as it filled Chandler's need to mother. He also acknowledges that Muriel cannot be a mother to him because she is still a child herself. She had married an older man hoping he would be the father she never had. And his father, likewise, married a woman who was a child. Accepting his own needs and family situation, Harvey begins to take action to help develop the relationship he desires with his parents. Instead of lamenting his mother's lack of attention toward him, he accepts her for who she is and, to her surprise, begins to respond to her with warmth. He also reaches out to his father by making a luncheon engagement with him at his club. When Mr. Beaumont congratulates him on the publication of his horror story, Harvey is touched by his sincere approval.

The final step in this process of transformation is letting go of the carnival in his mind. Harvey's carnival fantasy symbolizes several aspects of his life. It is an attempt to stave off loneliness with colored lights and bright costumes, cheerful music, and happy crowds. It is vaguely associated with a feeling of love from his mother and, even more vaguely, with their laughing together. The carnival also represents a carefree life to which he would like to escape. It is the childhood he never had. Relinquishing this comforting fantasy shows he has accepted reality and is starting to come to terms with it. Harvey makes this break with the carnival after Chandler leaves for Detroit. As he waits for sleep, in his own bed in the Fifth Avenue apartment, the carnival approaches. But this time the carnival people wave good-bye to him, turn, and travel the other way. Harvey falls asleep as his imaginary carnival disappears from his mind forever.

Because Harvey's carnival fantasy is so real to him, the scenes he imagines are filled with strong imagery. It is easy to see the whirl of colored lights, hear the tinny carousel music, and smell the sawdust and popcorn. And amidst all this happy confusion, walks Harvey, the Tallest Man in the World. Wersba also evokes vivid imagery when she describes the Fifth Avenue apartment with the dogs sitting on the expensive but shabby couches watching the evening news on television. It is almost possible to hear the thuds of dogs running up and down the apartment's long hallway, chasing a toy Harvey has thrown, and to empathize with the family in the apartment below, whose only alternative to living beneath a dog kennel is to sell their apartment to wealthy Muriel Beaumont.

In addition to canine noises, *The Carnival in My Mind* resounds with the diverse voices of its human characters. Chandler, who calls everyone "darling," speaks with a dramatic intensity befitting a theater hopeful. Because she is kind and well intentioned, the silkiness of her voice often masks the deceptive web in which she lives. Holmes is also kind, but his strong sense of decorum and the formality with which he speaks usually conceal his genuine affection for Harvey.

Nicholas Ormolu, the doorman, is also formal when he speaks to Harvey, but he is seldom kind to him. Although he gives Harvey helpful information in the beginning of the story about how to locate Chandler, he responds to Harvey's "thank you" with "I wish I could say it was my pleasure, but it has not been my pleasure. You have taken up ten minutes of my time" (35). His criminal background seems evident in the discrepancy between his polite manner and his harsh words. Harvey later gathers the confidence to tell Mr. Ormolu he is a nice man but a bully. Tommy the dog walker, on the other hand, is outrightly rude to Harvey, announcing that he is 10 minutes late bringing the dogs down for their walk. When Harvey explains that it "couldn't be helped" because he had to get the dogs' raincoats on, Tommy snaps, "I don't care if it can be helped or not. I am now late for Mrs. Bolt's Schnauzers" (53). He then barks commands that the seven Irish setters obey immediately, and they are off for their daily walk in Central Park. Muriel seldom speaks to Harvey, but when she does she is terse and impatient, implying she would rather not have to deal with him. Mr. Beaumont's voice is rarely heard, but when he speaks to Harvey in their Connecticut home, his words are direct, although his manner is vague, making communication with his son difficult.

Surrounded by all these distinct voices, if Harvey were not narrating this story, his own voice might seem rather indistinct because of his lack of self-confidence and because he really is not a center of attention in his family. But although his situation is inherently sad, the circumstances causing his unhappy state are so bizarre and the people with whom he shares his world are so extraordinary that Harvey's story is funny and, in the end, uplifting. Harvey generally speaks as a serious, despondent young man, but his inner voice conveys amusing imaginary scenarios. For example, he envisions his mother, newly decorated by the Irish Setter Improvement Club of North America, leading a regiment of uniformed Irish setters into battle against the dreaded enemy—people. Muriel Beaumont is certainly eccentric, but her unhappy childhood, spent in boarding schools, makes her almost pitiable. Her behavior is so extreme—giving seven dogs the run of a Fifth Avenue apartment, hiring a dietitian to prepare their meals, sending out engraved litter announcements, scolding Harvey for letting them watch TV horror movies because viewing violence is bad for dogs—that she is entertaining in her eccentricity. Harvey's own fascination with horror stories also adds a comical dimension to the novel. In the film his mother forbids the dogs to watch, a deadly virus has grown to one hundred trillion times its normal size and this huge bug is creeping through the streets of New York, sending people scurrying in all directions. The stories Harvey writes are so morbid, "filled with people who are pecked to death by falcons [and] gangsters who murdered their victims by baking them into enormous loaves of French bread" (29), that they are laughable, thereby enabling Wersba to parody another literary genre.

The Carnival in My Mind is Wersba's favorite among her novels because it "reflects [her] life in the theater." The character of Chandler Brown is based on a flamboyant girl she knew at prep school. This girl was terrifically theatrical, exaggerated in a Tallulah Bankhead way, and quite grown-up, even at 17. She went on to become a theatrical costume designer, but she always stuck in Wersba's mind as an intriguing character. After a 30-year interval, she emerged as Chandler Brown, much to Wersba's delight. Through Harvey's observations about Chandler, Wersba imparts her belief that actors have an insatiable need to be loved and admired. Writers, Harvey reflects, may need to shine as well, but perhaps not as desperately. *Carnival* also draws upon Wersba's familiarity with and affection for other parts of New York City besides Greenwich Village. Harvey and Chandler frequent such places as Tiffany's, Cartier's, Saks Fifth Avenue, the St. Regis Hotel, the Dorset Hotel, the Plaza Hotel, and the Metropolitan Museum of Art.

Wersba also likes *Carnival* because she is fond of the metaphor. She has no idea where the carnival idea came from, but it might be connected with the tiny circus in *Let Me Fall Before I Fly,* her favorite among the books she has written for children. In any case, Wersba was pleased every time the carnival entered into the story and thoroughly enjoyed writing about it. She still relishes it just as she does the book's ending, when Harvey bids farewell to the childhood he always wanted but never will have. He does this on the same day he says good-bye to Chandler.

The character of Muriel Beaumont is based on an actual person who was the president and sole member of the Irish Setter Rescue League of America. Wersba came in contact with her after buying a starved Irish setter from a street person on Fifth Avenue. It was most likely that this young dog, which Wersba called Bridie, had been stolen. Wersba cared for Bridie while trying to locate her owner. Unfortunately, Wersba was unable to train her, and Bridie was often exuberantly out of control. Wersba eventually found a man willing to adopt Bridie, but she had dearly loved this "cheerful monster" and missed her terribly. Much of what she learned from her experiences with this Irish setter is incorporated in *Carnival,* and writing this novel helped Wersba console herself while grieving the loss of her dog.

Reviewers responded warmly to *The Carnival in My Mind*. Paul Heins praised Wersba in *Horn Book* for the "considerable sympathetic humor" she used in creating a "gallery of unconventional characters" and for being "unabashedly frank" while "avoiding the sordid."[7] Most reviewers considered the characters believable, but one questioned whether a mother could really not notice her son's absence.[8] Many noted the book's clear appeal to teens.

Crazy Vanilla

In *Crazy Vanilla* Wersba introduces Tyler Woodruff, another lonely teenage boy, 14 years old, and also from an affluent family. For the past two years, Tyler and his mother have been living in their country home in North Haven, located in the cluster of small towns on the eastern tip of Long Island called the Hamptons. Mr. Woodruff, a brilliant Wall Street stockbroker, lives in the family's New York City apartment during the week and resides in North Haven on weekends. Although most people view the Hamptons as "one big cocktail party surrounded by water,"[9] the area is actually a paradise for wild birds and provides Tyler abundant opportunities to pursue his one joy in life, wildlife photography. Tyler's passion for photography, however, angers his father, who considers bird photography an effeminate pastime. George Woodruff has already banished his eldest son, Cameron, for being gay and refuses to buy camera equipment for Tyler or pay for film processing.

Cameron, with whom Tyler has always been exceptionally close despite the seven-year difference in their ages, is the only person who truly appreciates Tyler's talent for photography. When they both lived in New York, Cameron served as a buffer between Tyler—who has always been socially isolated—and the other boys at Spencer School. But Cameron now studies at the Institute of Design in New York, so when Tyler's schoolmates at Southampton Country-Day ridicule Tyler, calling him "the Birdman of Alcatraz" and intensifying his perception that "a teenager who is different pays a price" (37), he feels more alone than ever. Although the brothers have been forbidden to see each other for the past two years, they speak weekly on the phone and occasionally arrange a secret rendezvous in the city. During one of these meetings, Cameron tells Tyler he has fallen in love with a man named Vincent Milanese and that they plan to live together. Although Tyler wants to hate Vincent, he finds him well mannered, cultured, and friendly. Tyler, realizing his relationship with his idolized older brother will never be the same, feels desperately alone and yearns for a friend who will share his interest in bird photography. Fortunately, his longing is fulfilled by Mitzi Gerrard.

Tyler first encounters 15-year-old Mitzi working at Olsen's Ice-Cream Parlor in Sag Harbor, when he learns "Crazy Vanilla," his entry for "Olsen's-Annual-Ice-Cream-Naming Contest" (16), has not won the $1,000 prize. Having counted on this prize money for the purchase of a longer camera lens, Tyler is vocal about his disappointment. Mitzi, a very short waitress with crew-cut red hair, tells him to leave or she will call the police. He next discovers her at the pond photographing swans with an inferior Kodak camera.

She shows great sensitivity toward the swans, which allow her to come surprisingly close. She is also keenly perceptive about people, realizing immediately that Tyler is depressed. Although their initial interactions are a bit truculent, Tyler and Mitzi soon become steadfast friends—an unusual relationship for these two offbeat loners who rarely develop friendships. Mitzi, who shares Tyler's plan to become a professional wildlife photographer, knows a great deal about both birds and photography. In addition, her frequent moves, owing to her mother's unsuccessful health-food store ventures, have shown her the tough side of life, sharpened her awareness of human nature, and made her uncommonly independent.

Mitzi and Tyler spend hours shooting pictures together and talking. Tyler expresses his distress about Cameron's homosexuality, his parents' fighting, his mother's drinking, and his father's rigidity. Wise beyond her years, Mitzi points out that Tyler is angry at Cameron because he misses him so much; she helps him understand his brother's homosexuality and encourages Tyler to forgive his brother for falling in love. Difficult as it is, Tyler is eventually able to reconnect with Cameron, who, of course, had never stopped caring about him. Mitzi also suggests that Tyler's mother, because of her gregarious nature, might benefit from AA meetings. Tyler slowly gathers the courage to give his mother AA literature, and they begin to attend open meetings together. Tyler is still uncomfortable around his father, but he does assert himself by hanging a portrait of his pet duck, Zeppo, on the living-room wall, and George Woodruff then perceives his son a little differently. His friendship with Mitzi changes the way Tyler sees himself and the world around him. He has accepted that being different can be advantageous and that life is probably not fair, but it doesn't matter. In the fall, when Mitzi, her mother, and her mother's faith-healer boyfriend pack up their meager possessions and move to Santa Fe, New Mexico, Tyler knows he will never see his friend again. He suspects Mitzi will remain a loner all her life, but her solitude will enable her to achieve her dreams. And he believes the same about himself.

Wersba explores various relationships in *Crazy Vanilla*. The friendship between Tyler and Mitzi is central to the story, and it forms the basis for Tyler's narrative. In addition to never having had a friend before, Tyler has attended all-male schools, so he has had little interaction with females his age. Mitzi is a good match for him not only because of their mutual interest in wildlife photography, but also because she is self-assured, clear about her values, and sensitive to other people. Tyler loves Mitzi, but because "physical things turn [her] off" ever since her mother's ex-boyfriend tried to rape her (141), their relationship remains platonic. Tyler's sexual inexperience coupled with his "good heart" (142) make him the ideal friend for Mitzi as well.

The relationships Mitzi and Tyler have with their mothers are not ideal, but they are viable in different ways. Mitzi takes care of Shirley Gerrard. She reminds her to take her blood-pressure medicine and protects her by not telling her about the attempted rape. She works long hours at Shirley's health-food store and gives her the money she makes at the ice-cream parlor and car wash. When Tyler complains that Shirley and her boyfriend take advantage of Mitzi by having her shop, cook, and run errands, Mitzi matter-of-factly responds, "I don't know what you're talking about, Woodruff. She's my *mother*" (136). He later learns that many years earlier, even though she was poverty stricken, Shirley had refused to give Mitzi up for adoption. Mitzi accepts her responsibilities without resentment, but she follows her own desires when it comes to eating junk food and smoking cigarettes.

Tyler and his mother also enjoy a compatible relationship. As Mitzi puts it, Katherine Woodruff dotes on Tyler. Tyler assumes this is what all mothers do. He knows she believes that everything he and Cameron do is wonderful, and he is touched when she tries to mollify his short-tempered father for the sake of her children. Katherine is a blond, vivacious, slightly plump, kind-hearted Alabama debutante who married well, but unfortunately can't do anything right as far as her husband is concerned. In many ways Tyler and Katherine are like two children intimidated by an overbearing father. Although he understands that his mother's "main relationship is not with people, but with alcohol" (11), he does not consider helping her until Mitzi suggests AA.

George Woodruff's main relationship is with money. A brilliant Wall Street broker, he is parsimonious and uses money as a means to control others. He tries to force Tyler to give up wildlife photography by cutting off financial support. Rigid and short-tempered, he is rarely contradicted. This is why Tyler's three ducks, Harpo, Groucho, and Zeppo, infuriate him. Although it is comical the way Zeppo, the female duck, takes a passion to George and follows him around "with an adoring look on her face" (26), George does not find it amusing. He is an uncompromising person who must control every situation. His father instilled perfectionism in him by "tortur[ing] him with high standards" and this perfectionism tends to drive him crazy (48). Fortunately, Tyler's psychological distance from his father will probably enable him to stage the revolt he needs to keep him from following in his father's footsteps.

Cameron's relationship with Vincent enables Wersba to address the topic of homosexuality. Bright, good-looking, artistically gifted, sociable, and caring, Cameron was a popular teenager. He knew he was gay from age 11 or 12 but, not wanting to be different, tried to deny it. He tells Tyler it is not immoral to be gay and explains he could not change his sexual orientation even if he wanted to. Mitzi points out that it takes courage to come out of the closet and that being gay can be advantageous because it makes you different. Cameron and Vincent make an enviably happy couple, thus providing a positive statement about committed homosexual relationships.

Although Tyler is capable of having satisfying human relationships, he still likes "birds better than people" (183). After Mitzi leaves, he returns to photography as a solitary endeavor. Interestingly, the gifts he and Mitzi exchange upon parting show that each knows what the other most needs to advance toward a career in photography. Tyler gives Mitzi the expensive, sophisticated camera equipment she requires to better capture wildlife on film. Mitzi knows it's not equipment that is impeding Tyler's development as a wildlife photographer, but his attitude toward wild animals. She knows that Tyler needs to stop sentimentalizing animals by focusing on the pretty side of nature. He must embrace the awesome and terrible aspects as well as the beautiful if his work is to be distinctive. To this end she gives him a magazine clipping containing a cherished Henry Beston quotation that emphasizes that animals are not incomplete or lesser beings to be measured against or patronized by humans: "They are not brethren, they are not underlings; they are other nations, caught with ourselves in the net of life and time, fellow prisoners of the splendor and travail of the earth" (qtd. 182).

Tyler has been working toward developing a dispassionate relationship with wildlife, and perhaps a more objective attitude will enable him to fulfill his dream of winning the *Wildlife International* nature photography contest. This accomplishment is more likely than realizing his dream of marrying Mitzi on a riverbank in the Serengeti and the two of them traveling all over the world on photography adventures. But even though his dreams about Mitzi won't come true, his relationship with her has helped Tyler believe in himself. He realizes that most people never get what they want out of life—his mother wanted to be an actress and his father wanted to be a doctor—and he knows it will be difficult for him to become a professional photographer. However, he now has Mitzi, who does not believe in obstacles, to inspire him as he works toward becoming an award-winning photographer.

Just as *The Carnival in My Mind* draws heavily upon Wersba's experiences living in New York City, *Crazy Vanilla* reflects her life when she first moved to North Haven. Like Tyler and Mitzi, Wersba became intrigued with photographing the wild birds that shared her environment. The pond where her characters photograph the swans is the pond at the end of her backyard. The Speedy Print Shop, Olsen's Ice-Cream Parlor, and the Cooper Hotel are all modeled after Sag Harbor establishments. Tyler's particular passion for swan photography is no coincidence, for Wersba has long been fascinated with swans. Accordingly, swans are central to this story not only because they make interesting photographic subjects but also for their symbolic significance in terms of Tyler and Mitzi's relationship. During the span of Tyler and Mitzi's friendship, Arnold, the swan who brought them together, grew from a cygnet into a huge homely bird—from an infant into an adolescent. He will soon be free and independent, just as Tyler and Mitzi will be when they become adults. But for now, all three are successfully struggling through the difficulties of adolescence.

Marijo Duncan, who reviewed *Crazy Vanilla* for *Voice of Youth Advocates (VOYA),* considered this novel "typical Wersba, complete with likable characters who handle tough growing up situations well, and with a sense of humor." She declared it "Wersba at her best and a superb addition to the world of realistic YA fiction."[10] Other reviewers commented on Wersba's excellence as a storyteller and her skill as a writer. *Kirkus* called it a "carefully wrought, unsentimental portrait of friendship."[11] The *Bulletin of the Center for Children's Books* said *Crazy Vanilla* "is written with perception and candor, has strong characterization, and is commendable in pace and structure."[12] As usual, there were some questions about the believability of the characters of Mitzi and Tyler, but for the most part *Crazy Vanilla* was well received by both American and British reviewers.

In these three novels Wersba has again created characters whose lives change for the better due to an improbable relationship. In the cases of Mrs. Woodfin and Albert Scully and Steven Harper and Hadley Norman, there is a large age difference, just as there is between J. F. McAllister and Harold Murth. The age discrepancy between Harvey and Chandler is also significant, but the one-year difference between Tyler and Mitzi does not seem to matter, even though she is the older one in the relationship. Harold Murth unwittingly alters J. F.'s life by providing a goal for an affluent teen who had previously been "completely selfish and spoiled" (107). Chandler changes Harvey's life by nurturing Harvey's writing dream. Mitzi transforms Tyler's life by sharing a philosophy that helps him overcome his anger and bitterness. All three characters—J. F., Harvey, and Tyler—come to accept themselves more fully because of these relationships, and this self-acceptance provides emotional balance as well as a more balanced view of life.

4. Unconventional Romance: The Saga of Rita Formica

Wersba's next three books, which she calls her Sag Harbor trilogy, chronicle the love story of Rita Formica and Arnold Bromberg. Sixteen-year-old Rita and 32-year-old Arnold meet in June and by Christmas they have become lovers, making theirs a June–December romance in several ways. Their story, as told by Rita herself, begins in *Fat: A Love Story* and continues in *Love Is the Crooked Thing* and *Beautiful Losers*.

Fat: A Love Story

Rita Formica is 16, fat, and short. At five foot three, she weighs 200 pounds. She has always been obese, even as a child, and her loving parents have spent thousands of dollars trying to help her control her weight. But Rita eats constantly. She consumes candy bars, Sara Lee cakes, ice-cream sandwiches, pizzas, cheeseburgers, strawberry malteds, jelly doughnuts, and Gummy Bears regularly and in large quantities. She is a frequent customer at the Heavenly Cafe in Sag Harbor, where her friend Nicole Sicard, who is 19, petite, beautiful, and French, works as a waitress. Needing a summer job to support her outrageous eating habits, Rita answers an ad for a delivery person and is hired to deliver Arnold Bromberg's cheesecakes by bicycle. Arnold operates his newly opened business from his home in the back of a defunct dog-grooming parlor not far from where Rita and her parents live in Sag Harbor.

Soon after accepting the job with Arnold, Rita catches sight of Robert Swann and immediately falls in love with this slim, beautiful, aristocratic Harvard graduate. Utterly infatuated with Robert, who is everything she is not, Rita joins the health club where he works out and tries to gain his attention. Her attempts fail miserably, as does her weight therapy with Dr. Marsha Strawberry. Rita decides to accept Nicole's offer of assistance. Nicole will be the "bait to catch the fish."[1] She will join the fitness club, become friends with Robert, introduce him to Rita, and then fade out of the picture. Unfortunately, this bait-and-switch strategy backfires, and Nicole and Robert become lovers.

Meanwhile Arnold's cheesecake business is failing, but he is elated to have Rita's daily company. The better Rita gets to know Arnold, the more impressed she is by his sensitivity, intelligence, musical talent, and eternal optimism. Depressed by the situation with Robert, Rita confides in Arnold, who listens sympathetically and expresses alarm that Robert does not see the beauty in her. When Rita learns that Nicole and Robert are engaged, she binges to the point of illness. Realizing she needs help, she turns to Arnold, who takes her into his home, shows her the type of kindness she has only known from her parents, and carefully listens to her. Rita reveals the entire history of her compulsive eating and her urge to kill herself over Robert and Nicole.

When she finishes, Arnold discloses that he was a fat person until he was 18 years old. He theorizes that Rita's fat is like an armor she purposefully maintains to "protect the fragile person within" (132). The way to rectify the situation is by simply "letting go" (133). Rita realizes this means letting go of Robert and Nicole, of food, and of her negative self-image. In addition, she recognizes something else: she has fallen in love with Arnold Bromberg. "I love you, Mr. Bromberg," she tells him. "I just didn't know it before" (134). This time her love is returned; for Arnold has been in love with Rita from the first moment they met.

After clarifying that their love for each other is not that of a father and child but of a man and a woman, Arnold and Rita begin an intense physical relationship. Their lovemaking is passionate, but limited because Arnold is old-fashioned and because

Rita is "sixteen and a virgin" and he is "thirty-two and not" (140). As they spend every moment they can together, their friendship continues to deepen. Arnold cooks special meals for Rita, who loses 40 pounds and feels much better about her appearance. Wanting a complete relationship with Arnold, Rita stages a temporary marriage ceremony on Christmas Eve in the Whalers Church. That night Rita and Arnold consummate their relationship. *Fat* ends on an upbeat note with Rita joining Arnold in his belief that there is a God and the universe is benevolent. Rita has changed philosophically, as well as physically and mentally, as a result of her relationship with Arnold.

The first in the trilogy, *Fat* introduces Rita and Arnold both to each other and to the audience. Spontaneous, kindhearted, and vulnerable, Rita is a remarkably engaging character. Her weight problem has made her a social misfit as well as amusing and skeptical. As she says, fat people really are jolly—"jolly as a means of avoiding suicide" (13). Thus Rita has long been the life of the party and popular with her peers at Peterson High School. Considering her an easy mark, boys try to take advantage of her sexually, but even though she has a pretty face, they never love her. Her parents, working-class year-round Sag Harbor residents, love Rita and do all they can for her, but it is not enough. In her loneliness, Rita longs for romance with the handsome, svelte, golden Robert Swann. Robert brings out Rita's penchant for daydreaming and fabricating stories. But even though fantasies such as "Skylar Cunningham," the persona she creates for herself, fail to lure Robert into loving her, they do demonstrate the vividness of Rita's imagination and make her desire to become a writer seem plausible. Arnold, to whom Rita presents her real self, values Rita for her abundant positive qualities and, believing she has the characteristics and temperament of a writer, encourages her to follow her literary aspirations.

Arnold understands a bit about writers because he almost completed a Ph.D. in literature and is writing a book on Bach. In addition, he plays the organ well, quotes poetry, loves all animals but is particularly fond of shorebirds, and believes "right action is always taking place" in a benevolent world (60). He was raised in

Kansas, where his father is a Presbyterian minister, but moved to Sag Harbor because he liked the name of the place. Tall, muscular, and large-boned, he has brown curly hair, is immaculately groomed, and wears sneakers even with his "clean, but shabby" business suits (110). Although his speech remains formal, he is kind and compassionate to all. Solitary by nature, he has many qualities that combine to make him "very odd and rare," what Nicole calls *"un original"* (26).

Although Arnold and Rita are the central characters in *Fat,* Wersba playfully creates supporting characters Robert Swann, Nicole Sicard, and Marsha Strawberry, who do not support Rita at all. Strawberry is of particular interest because she is an ineffectual therapist, similar in some regards to Dr. Waingloss in *Tunes.* This time, however, the theories expounded, and mildly mocked, concern weight problems. Rigid, egotistical, and humorless, Dr. Strawberry may be an inept weight therapist, but she functions successfully as Rita's foil. For example, the entries in the stream-of-consciousness journal Rita is required to keep are thoughtful and amusing, but Dr. Strawberry castigates her for being vulgar. She does not appreciate Rita comparing Robert to white cake with vanilla icing, "a cake both pure and sexual"; Arnold to a "deep and mysterious red wine"; and Nicole to a "passionate omelette" made with mushrooms and cheese (118). When Rita decides to play it straight and confesses to cheating on her diet, Marsha becomes cold and insulting. The result of their dysfunctional relationship is the reader's deeper understanding and augmented cheering for Rita as she struggles with intense loneliness and obesity. Measured against Robert Swann's ungraciousness, Nicole's betrayal, and Marsha's lack of compassion, it is easy to see why Rita falls in love with Arnold—oddball, loner, and impractical dreamer that he is.

Love Is the Crooked Thing

In *Love Is the Crooked Thing,* Rita's parents are alarmed to learn that Rita is having sex with a man they consider a 32-year-old loser. Arnold agrees that he is not good for Rita and departs, leaving behind a note telling Rita he will love her into eternity. Baffled by Arnold's departure, angry at her parents, and lonelier than ever, Rita again starts to overeat and regains some of the weight she lost when Arnold was helping her diet. She also begins to write every day, as Arnold has said professional writers do whether they feel like it or not. She first composes poetry, and then in the spring she begins an improbable novel called *Rosamund*. *Rosamund* takes place in France and involves a married couple named Robert and Nicole. Nicole, it turns out, is a bigamist, and Robert commits suicide by walking into the sea with Rosamund, with whom he slept before he realized she was his long-lost twin sister. From the cryptic postcards Arnold has been sending over the last several months, Rita realizes he is living in Zürich, Switzerland. Deciding she must visit him, if only for a weekend, she attempts to finance the trip by writing a hack romance. With the first 20 pages of *Rosamund* as a writing sample, Rita visits Doris Morris, a Sag Harbor resident who used to work at the local dry cleaner's until she struck it rich writing historical romances under the pseudonym of Amanda Starcross.

Having gone from rags to riches, Doris is now an agent who assigns romances, westerns, and detective novels to a "stable" of writers who take her plots and her assistant's historical research and fill in the lurid details. Having never read a bodice ripper, Rita studies the form by reading six Starcross novels and trying to imitate the style. Rita's writing is not sexy enough, but figuring she will catch on eventually, Doris assigns Rita her first "Starcross" book, *Savage Sunset*. As Rita noted earlier, most of Amanda Starcross's books have the word "savage" in their titles. Rita struggles with her book, but the $3,000 it will bring and her desire to see Arnold lure her on. She accepts a date with Jerry Malone, who writes the "Victor Colorado" westerns for Doris Morris, hoping he will provide some writing tips. Jerry/Victor's advice is the same as Doris/Amanda's: sex—and the sooner the better. This is also how Jerry feels about his relationship with Rita because, although she doesn't know it yet, "fat girls turn [him] on."[2]

Fearing she cannot fulfill her contract, Rita decides to offer Jerry sex (and half the money) if he will write her novel for her. She will be like a heroine in a Starcross novel; she will sacrifice her body for the sake of love, yet remain pure in her heart. It seems reasonable to do this for the man she loves. Jerry's ego is wounded when Rita makes her cold-blooded offer, but he agrees to write the book for $1,000; the sex part, he says, is "a real turn off" (82), and he never takes her up on it. He does write the book, but Rita is appalled by the historical inaccuracies and misrepresentations he includes, many of which he concocts while smoking marijuana. Feeling the horrendous book is her responsibility, Rita confesses the whole scheme to Doris Morris. When Doris asks why she needs the money, Rita describes her love affair with Arnold. Touched by the pathos in Rita's story, especially Arnold's departure, Doris gives Rita a check for $2,500 to pay off Jerry and cover her trip to Zürich.

With the help of her good friend in New York, Corry Brown, who covers for her and assists in the arrangements, Rita arrives in Zürich on 30 August, Arnold's birthday. The cabdriver takes her to the Utoquai, an embankment where people sit and watch swans, which appears in many of Arnold's postcards. Rita waits for hours, and as she suspected, Arnold eventually comes to feed the swans. He is overjoyed to see her and she ends up staying five days in Zürich. Rita learns that Arnold begins each day by watching the sun rise over the Zürichsee, then listens to a brilliant organist practice at the Fraumünster, after which he goes to the library and works on his book about Bach. He seems content leading the life of a frugal scholar; he is also more sophisticated than when he left her seven months ago.

Although their love affair is rekindled, Arnold tells her nothing has changed and they have no future together. Rita realizes that even though Arnold does love and value her, he is unable to commit to marriage, and that is why he originally pursued their unlikely relationship. She understands she does not have to be dependent on Arnold to lose weight. And she knows she will always love him. Although she departs not knowing what will become of their relationship, Rita is inspired to write a book, a *real* romance, the love story of Rita Formica and Arnold Bromberg. Writing this book will save, even redeem her. It will help her make sense of her life.

Rita's desire to write love stories and Doris Morris's stable of hack writers enable Wersba to satirize the phenomenon of the historical romance. As Doris tells Rita, she and her writers turn out a "product like cornflakes or vitamin-B enriched white bread. T. S. Eliot we are not" (32). At the heart of the genre is "erotic romance. The kind that doesn't really exist, but the kind that every woman wants" (33). Doris explains that the plots all follow a formula:

> Early in the book, the girl—who is always a headstrong type—loses her virginity to some gorgeous, mysterious, slightly cruel man. By the end of the book she has *tamed* this man and he has come to adore her. But first there's got to be a lot of complication and misunderstanding, the hero estranged from the heroine, and she estranged from him, and so on. Sometimes, a second man comes into the picture—a type who is noble but dull—and often there's a second woman too, as a contrast to the heroine. The sex has got to be erotic without porn. (34–35)

To Doris's description Rita adds, "The women have ash-blond or raven hair, are breathtakingly beautiful, and the men make love like they have just been through a course with Masters and Johnson" (36). She notes the abundance of wish fulfillment as sex is described "symphonically," meaning "violins and flutes play when people have orgasms. White doves, metaphorically speaking, are released into the air" (36).

Rita feels conflicted about this type of writing; she is in love herself and her experience with passion is nothing like what these books describe. She asks Doris why all the sexual encounters are part seduction, part rape. Doris replies, "A woman's fantasy is to lose control with someone who cares for her." Being overpowered means the woman "doesn't have to take the responsibility for her feelings. Sex without guilt, it's called" (41–42).

Rita's friend Corry Brown has no conflict about the genre at all. She considers it completely antifeminist because women are victims, forced into sex and enslaved by their rapists. Regarding historical romance as soft porn because the books are "written to arouse," she condemns them as "the opiate of the housewife" (63). Corry complains that these steamy, antifeminist novels are "putting the movement back a hundred years" (50).

Examples of Rita's unsuccessful attempts to write *Savage Sunset*—which is about a female spy in the Civil War who tries to seduce President Abraham Lincoln—and the excerpts she and Doris read from the other lurid novels not only contribute information about the genre of historical romance, but they also add humor to Wersba's novel. Doris openly admits the writing is terrible, but matter-of-factly states that that's the genre, take it or leave it. Doris is pragmatic in her approach to writing, but she is a likable character who doesn't take herself or her "profession" too seriously. Her kindness toward Rita and her overall attitude soften Wersba's criticism—if not of the genre itself, at least of some of the people who make a living writing it. Not everyone is an opportunist of Jerry Malone's caliber.

Juxtaposed with passages about heaving bosoms and swelling manhood à la historical romance are memories of poems Arnold used to recite to Rita such as Yeats's "Brown Penny" from which *Love Is the Crooked Thing* takes its title. According to the poet contemplating the wonderful, mysterious complexity of love, "There is nobody wise enough / To find out all that is in it, / For he would be thinking of love / Till the stars had run away / And the shadows eaten the moon" (qtd. 67). Rita's world is also filled with images of Zürich that arise from the travel literature she reads to acquaint herself with Arnold's new home. The River Limmat, the Zürichsee, the Fraumünster, the Utoquai, and Old Town all become realities when she visits Arnold and he shows her the medieval city that enchants him. Wersba's familiarity with and love of Zürich are apparent when she describes the city, adding realistic details much as she does when the story is set in Sag Harbor.

Beautiful Losers

Ten months after Rita visits him in Zürich, Arnold returns to Sag Harbor and *Beautiful Losers* begins. In the meantime, Rita, who is now 18 and a high-school graduate, has definitely decided to forgo college and become a writer. Her career begins when she accepts a job writing a hospital newsletter. At night she works on her novel, *All the Slow Dances,* which is the love story of Rita Formica and Arnold Bromberg. Then after a 10-month silence, Arnold begins to write her beautiful, poetry-filled love letters. When she does not answer his letters, Arnold decides to return to Sag Harbor. Rita's parents are disappointed when they learn she had secretly turned down the colleges that had accepted her. However, they are astounded to learn Rita visited Arnold in Zürich last summer, and that he is now returning. Tony Formica stomps out of the house, but Mrs. Formica ruefully accepts Rita's intention to reunite with Arnold. After all, she herself married Tony against the wishes of her parents when she was 19. But when they hear Rita will be spending the night at a motel with Arnold, you'd think "I had murdered the Pope," writes Rita.[3]

Arnold wants to get married right away, but now Rita is unsure. Sensing that Arnold wants to marry her out of loneliness, she suggests they live together first. Once again Rita's parents are distraught. Her father cuts her off financially and tells her not to come back when the affair is over. Rita tells him she does not want his money, just his understanding, and leaves. Soothing herself with a double malted at the Heavenly Cafe, Rita realizes that her father is angry because he has spent so much money on her, and her choosing to go her own way means his investment has not paid off.

Poor but deeply in love, Rita and Arnold rent a run-down beach cottage, which they call the Ferry House in honor of the Shelter Island ferry that regularly crosses the channel from a nearby dock. Doris Morris loans them some furniture; they purchase inexpensive linens and blankets; and they buy used kitchenware at the thrift shop. Clean but still in ill-repair, the Ferry House becomes their home on 1 September. Because their finances are running low, Rita takes on a series of temporary jobs to supplement her income from the "Hospital News." Between riding her Honda moterbike from job to job and doing domestic errands, she has no time to work on *All the Slow Dances.* Arnold does the cooking and continues to work on the book he is writing about Bach. Although Rita phones her mother daily, she seldom sees her. The one time Mrs. Formica comes for tea, she tells Arnold she and Mr. Formica do not approve of him or the living arrangement he and Rita have.

Rita is upset when her motorbike is stolen, but Arnold assures her everything will be all right. When she questions his ability to remain so calm, he explains the Zen philosophy of letting go of the past and living in the moment. Rita lives in the moment for a while, riding a dilapidated bicycle to her new second job as assistant to the children's writer Nora Thurston Quadrangle, whom she calls the Dragon Lady. However, Rita eventually becomes frustrated because she is supporting Arnold, as well as doing most of the household work, and not getting any writing done. The exuberant, untrained puppy Arnold gives her for Christmas is the last straw. She and Arnold argue, and, at his suggestion, she moves back in with her parents. After a trial separation allows them time to think, Arnold asks Rita to return. This time things are different: he has taken a job as an organist and choirmaster and is studying bookbinding; he has sold part of his antique magazine collection to buy them a car; and he has made their house more livable. They decide to marry in the spring. Rita's parents have recently responded to Arnold's invitation to be part of their lives and have even come to appreciate him for the talented, if unusual, man he is. The story ends as Rita and Arnold are married aboard the Shelter Island ferry.

Rita and Arnold grow tremendously in *Beautiful Losers*. They both have revelations about themselves and committed relationships, and they realize the importance of fulfilling one's dreams. Rita's insights begin when she is bedridden with a bad cold and listens to radio talk show host Dr. Goforth provide instant psychotherapy. One caller, named Anne, finds herself unfulfilled at the age of 40 after doing everything right for her husband and children. Even though her children are successful and her husband still loves her, she remembers that as a teenager she wanted to be a clown in the Ringling Brothers Circus and make people laugh. Dr. Goforth has no answers for her, but Rita understands what Anne is saying. She envisions Anne as a dutiful housewife attending to her family's needs, but "in her mind would be the most wonderful circus in the world," in which Anne "in an incredible clown suit, her nose red and bulbous, a fright wig on her head, [would be] running around the ring with all the other clowns, tumbling, pratfalling, making people laugh" (99). Anne did not pursue her dream, and now she feels dissatisfied. Rita believes Anne should have heeded her heart and become a clown. Anne is like Rita's father, who is a good father but whose drinking problem and propensity for weeping probably indicate unhappiness. At 18 he wanted to be a race-car driver, but settled for a career as an auto mechanic. People such as her father and Anne help Rita realize that following one's dreams is essential if one is to be happy.

At the time Arnold suggests they separate in December to gain perspective on their relationship, Rita can't imagine him taking care of himself. But Arnold reminds her that she is not his mother. She notes that she is not his child either, but realizes she doesn't know who she is in the relationship. At home with her parents she recognizes not only how spoiled she was as a child, but how much of themselves her parents invested in her. This time she does not think in terms of monetary investments, but of their "hopes, dreams, vicarious feelings, fantasies" (123). They had lived their lives through her, and she would never be the "pretty college freshman, soon to marry a handsome college boy" that they wanted (124). Knowing she can only be herself, Rita accepts her parents' desires for her as both sad and wonderful because they never give up on her, hoping against hope that the weight she lost and her separation from Arnold mean she is heading for the future they had planned for her.

Rita knows that when she lived with Arnold she was a shrew, someone who argued over petty materialistic matters and failed to see the bigger picture of life. Her self-image suffers badly from this negative transformation. By sacrificing too much of herself within the relationship, she made herself unhappy and, therefore, difficult to live with. Understanding the importance of a commitment to oneself as well as to a marriage partner, Rita realizes that she wants for Arnold what *she* wants: the "freedom to be oneself." Marriage, as she read somewhere, means being the "guardian of another person's solitude" and allowing that person to "grow and change" (133). Rita is now prepared to face the challenge of commitment to herself, to Arnold, and to their relationship.

During their separation Arnold, too, reflected upon the nature of their relationship. He is still an idealist, "a man who lived for beauty, and who [is] sweet and gentle into his very soul" (6). But as he puts it, "Changes *needed* to be made in our lives. It's just that I'd never lived with anyone before. I didn't know what was required" (139). He recognizes that some material possessions, like another bureau and a car, can make life more comfortable for them. To this end he sells his rare magazine collection, takes a part-time job, and begins learning a trade. His actions show Rita that he has the courage to grow as their circumstances necessitate.

Rita's parents also grow within the course of the novel. They finally understand that Rita will not live her life according to their dreams. They also accept Arnold's invitation to be part of the life he and Rita are shaping for themselves. The two couples work together fixing up the Ferry House and visit each other for Sunday dinners. Arnold elicits Tony's advice on house and car repairs, making Tony feel involved in their lives. Tony does not weep as he did throughout the other two novels, and his drinking problem is not mentioned. Rita ceases to reject her mother's offers of furniture and appliances and enjoys the homey touches her mother adds to their simple abode. They are an extended family whose changing relationships afford each of them opportunities for growth.

Arnold and Rita are dreamers seemingly destined to fulfill their dreams. Even if Arnold never actually finishes his book on Bach, he is still a writer, as well as a philosopher, a musician, a painter, and a photographer; and he will have lived life by his own terms and his own standards of decency. To help Rita achieve her writing goal, Rita and Arnold agree to rise at dawn and work on their books daily. Now Rita's manuscript no longer lies in the drawer while she works to support Arnold. As the Sag Harbor trilogy is actually *All the Slow Dances,* Rita's writing dream is well under way. And she likes the way her life translates into fiction, saying:

> It was a good novel, the story of Arnold and me, and I liked every single thing about it. Told in the first person, it is the story of a small-town girl who falls in love with a man who can only be called *un original.* The man is older than the girl, and poverty-stricken, and the parents disapprove. There are scenes in Europe, after the man has taken flight. I had made him a painter instead of a writer, and I had changed a few other things too, but it was definitely autobiographical. (129)

Rita's is a true love story—not the fabricated kind she tried to produce as "Amanda Starcross"—but a genuine love story in which people care about one another and work out their differences. Rita's story offers hope for both young couples and their parents. As Arnold suspected, Rita has the soul of a writer.

Having aspiring writer Rita work for Nora Thurston Quadrangle (the Dragon Lady, who writes children's books about happy appliances), allows Wersba to have a little fun with writers who write purely for profit. By studying the market, Miss Quadrangle learns that books about toasters, eggbeaters, and vacuum cleaners provide potentially profitable heroes. Research, she explains, shows that young children are attracted to appliances, perhaps because machines are powerful and children are not. As a hardworking book machine, Quadrangle represents the inequities of success in the literary world: talented, aesthetic writers like Arnold and Rita will not necessarily succeed. But although the 30-plus books Quadrangle has published about good little appliances have made her a fortune, she is nevertheless lonely and unhappy. Rita's initial dislike of Miss Quadrangle softens when she discovers the Dragon Lady's vulnerability, and she eventually sees her in a more sympathetic light. When Rita tells Miss Quadrangle she plans to marry, the children's writer is sincerely happy for her and gives her a check for $500 as a wedding gift.

The issue of obesity is still present in this third novel. As Rita well knows, "one of the burdens of being fat is that everyone feels he or she has a right to comment on it" (53). Housewives are always trying to tell her what diet to try. Christopher, a high-school classmate, reacts to Rita as all males have since she reached puberty: she is first and foremost a fat girl—rather than intelligent, funny, or original. In all sincerity Christopher wants Rita to know about a ranch in the West, where fat women are put to sleep for six months to lose weight. Rita wonders why they just don't murder the women, "death is the ultimate diet, after all. Corpses lose weight like crazy" (21). Arnold values her for herself, but Rita understands that "the concept that thin equals no problems and no rejections is crazy" (53). Losing 40 pounds did not stop Arnold from leaving Rita for Switzerland. Rita decides to be herself, fat as she may be, and stop trying to conform to society's images of what women should look like.

Wersba recalls that the Sag Harbor trilogy was written during a period when she herself was attempting to lose weight. She was trying every crazy diet and attending all types of weight-loss clinics. About this time she became intrigued with steamy formula romances because one of her friends was doing some editing for a company that mass-produced these popular books—hence the character of Doris Morris in *Love Is the Crooked Thing.* Wersba selected Zürich as Rita and Arnold's rendezvous point because she had accompanied her friend Zue to Switzerland several times and was particularly fond of Zürich. She did not base the characters of Rita and Arnold on any particular people, but she got so attached to them she had trouble letting their story end.[4]

All three novels draw heavily upon Wersba's Sag Harbor surroundings. Many of the locations and establishments are based on actual places. Wersba can point out the abandoned cottage where she envisions Rita and Arnold lived, the church where Arnold played the organ, and the ferry on which they were married. She can also show visitors the ice-cream parlor and cafe Rita frequented, the hotel where Victor Colorado took her for dinner, and the room over the health-food store where he lived. One assumes this is the same health-food store Mitzi's mother, from *Crazy Vanilla,* once operated. The wild birds, especially the swans that frequently grace the novels, are particular favorites of Wersba's, and she delights in their presence. The *Southampton Press,* Sag Harbor's local paper, did an article on Wersba when *Fat* was first released and later printed a lengthy review of *Love Is the Crooked Thing.* In an earlier review of *Crazy Vanilla,* the paper was particularly interested in Wersba's portrayal of Sag Harbor and made it clear locals were delighted to have Wersba writing about the community.[5]

Other reviews showed favorable acceptance of the Sag Harbor trilogy. Diane Roback of *Publishers Weekly* applauded the unexpected happy ending in *Fat* along with Wersba's characteristic balancing of humor and pathos as she departs from her customary tale of unusual characters who love each other briefly and then part.[6] Some reviewers questioned the probability of the June–December relationship, noted the lack of objection on the part of Rita's parents, or mentioned problems with the plot, but most agreed with Hazel Rochman of *Booklist* that in *Fat: A Love Story* Wersba has created sympathetic characters and that "Rita's wry, sometimes desperate, voice carries the narrative."[7]

Rochman does not praise *Love Is the Crooked Thing* as highly, commenting that among other shortcomings the sequel "lacks the force and intensity of *Fat* though it has some of the same sweet poignancy." However, she concludes, "thinking romance fans will enjoy Wersba's funny and compassionate exploration of love, sex, and selfhood."[8] *Publishers Weekly* reviewer Roback seemed disappointed that Wersba did not provide a happy ending to Rita and Arnold's story after all and hopes "another sequel is in the works."[9] Reviewers generally disagreed about whether *Love Is the Crooked Thing* was inferior to *Fat,* quite a few believing *Love Is the Crooked Thing* to be even better than its prequel, but the consensus seems to be that the sexual explicitness in this book makes it best suited for mature teens or adults.

Beautiful Losers, according to Rochman's review in *Booklist,* contains some funny episodes but does not have the "sustained comedy and pathos of *Fat,* and Wersba overdoes the 'beautiful losers' message." Rochman did note, however, that realism and romance blended in this final installment of the trilogy.[10] Indeed, the efficacy of the book's realism formed the focus of many reviewers' remarks. Praising Wersba for her "integrity and heartbreaking honesty," Roback of *Publishers Weekly* found the ending to *Beautiful Losers* "very happy and very real" and very satisfying because Wersba "humorously melded the realistic with the romantic."[11] Eleanor K. MacDonald wrote in *School Library Journal* that "Wersba has realistically portrayed the conflict between conventional society and unusual lovers."[12] Considering the trilogy as a whole, Cathi Edgerton of *VOYA* commented that Rita and Arnold's is a real love story, "laced with warmth, humor, spirit, and optimism."[13]

The saga of Rita Formica is a departure from Wersba's previous story lines. For although Rita and Arnold are both outsiders with artistic dispositions who change each other's lives, their paths do not cross only once, but will instead intertwine for life. During her involvement with Arnold, Rita outgrows her obsessions with weight and schoolgirl crushes, matures in her relationship with her parents, weathers the disappointments of love, and begins to understand the complexities inherent in relationships. She has made the normal transition from adolescence to adulthood in a way that will enable her to continue her unconventional romance with a worthy man who is clearly *un original*. Rita's determination offers hope: It is possible to shape one's life according to passion and aspiration. Satisfaction in love and work need not follow conventional formulas.

5. Caring for Strays: The Tales of Heidi Rosenbloom

Wersba's next trilogy chronicles several years of the life of Heidi Rosenbloom in *Just Be Gorgeous, Wonderful Me,* and *The Farewell Kid.* Heidi, a kindhearted loner, cares first for a homeless street dancer, then adopts a dog needing a home, and eventually operates a dog rescue service. She also falls in love with three very different men.

Just Be Gorgeous

Without looks or talent, personality or intellect, what should a person do? wonders 16-year-old Heidi Rosenbloom.[1] Her mother, Shirley, envisions Heidi as a future Marilyn Monroe, and her father, Leonard, sees her as an Albert Einstein; but Heidi, who considers herself a nondescript teenage klutz, has no idea what she wants for herself. Affluent, lonely, and unhappy, she connects with none of the cliques at Spencer School, and her best friend has recently moved to California. In addition, her divorced parents make her feel like a Ping-Pong ball in their tempestuous relationship. Shirley has devoted herself to Heidi, and until she was 13, Heidi believed it was normal for a mother to be obsessed with her daughter's appearance. Now Heidi wears a secondhand, man's overcoat in an attempt to show that the compliant daughter whose mother tried to mold her into a virginal femme fatale is emerging as her own person. The thrift-shop overcoat annoys Shirley, but she still intends to control Heidi's appearance. Exasperated with a mother who refuses to allow her to develop her own selfhood, Heidi has her long, dark, curly hair cropped into a crew cut. The effect is perfect: Shirley is horrified.

Soon after shedding her locks, Heidi encounters Jeffrey Collins, who has bleached blond hair and wears a woman's fur jacket, tap dancing on the streets of New York. Following an impulse, Heidi invites Jeffrey for a cup of coffee. As the cup of coffee turns into two hamburgers and pie à la mode, Heidi learns that Jeffrey is unlike anyone she has ever known. He is 20 years old, gay, and homeless. Orphaned at birth, he was raised in foster homes and orphanages. A nun at one orphanage encouraged him to learn tap dancing by watching old movies. Hoping to be discovered and become a Broadway star, as well as to avoid getting beat up by Chicago "fag bash[ers]" (44), Jeffrey came to New York six months ago. Although he now sleeps in an abandoned building and lives off the coins people throw in his hat, he has "complete and utter faith" (47) that he will be discovered by a Broadway agent or producer. Jeffrey appreciates Heidi's unconventional appearance and encourages her to believe in herself. Touched by his optimism and acutely aware that he is starving, Heidi invites Jeffrey to dinner on the following Friday.

After Jeffrey comes to dinner, Shirley forbids Heidi to see him again, so her friendship with him becomes clandestine. Heidi accompanies Jeffrey to open auditions—at which he is always rejected, visits the abandoned building where he sleeps, and invites him to stay at her posh apartment when her mother is out of town. Heidi is in love with Jeffrey, but knows he loves her only as a sister or a very good friend. Thinking she might assist him in getting a Broadway part, Heidi asks Miss Margolis, the drama teacher at Spencer, to watch Jeffrey dance. After observing Jeffrey's sidewalk performance, Miss Margolis gently tells Heidi that although Jeffrey is a very good dancer, he lacks that "something extra" (131) to set him apart from the multitude of boys who want to break into show business. Heidi now believes that Jeffrey needs her more than ever.

One spring day when Heidi and Jeffrey are sitting in Central Park, Heidi spies a terrier. She instinctively knows it is homeless and needs her desperately. After the dog wolfs down Jeffrey's hamburger, Heidi declares she "*love*[s] this dog" (137) and is going to keep him. Naming him Happy, she considers him an omen for her future. She explains to Jeffrey, "I keep feeling that whatever I'm going to do with my life will involve dogs. And here we suddenly have a dog. Out of the blue." Jeffrey laughs and replies, "All you need, my darling, is another stray. First me, and then Happy." Heidi, slightly embarrassed, informs him she can love them both (138).

Jeffrey may have been playfully sarcastic, but in actuality a dog is just what Heidi does need. Happy first helps Heidi by causing her to realize that her mother does love her. When Heidi tells Shirley she needs a dog so that she will have someone to love her, Shirley quietly says, "No one has ever loved a child as much as I love you. . . . And if you don't know it, you're a fool" (141). Stunned by her mother's genuine pain, Heidi realizes Shirley and Leonard may not understand her, but they do love her. She, in turn, feels love and compassion for them, knowing each of them has had difficult parental relationships in their own lives.

Happy also helps Heidi several months later when a gay couple befriends Jeffrey, causing her to feel left out of his life. Heidi responds by devoting herself to Happy, the first living being she has ever been able to call her own. Happy not only makes her feel needed but also provides a peaceful means for staging the revolution she requires to become independent of her mother. When Jeffrey and his new friends move to Hollywood, hoping to work in movies, Happy continues to need her. Heidi knows she will never hear from Jeffrey again, but he has helped her gain a feeling of self-worth. Moreover, her relationship with him has enabled Heidi to realize that "sometimes you fall in love with the wrong person and don't even know it. Sometimes you give your future away, rather than keeping it for yourself" (156). Fortunately, she still has her future to look forward to, and she can share it with Happy.

But what shall she do with her future? Heidi has already accepted, thanks to the eternally optimistic Jeffrey, the ideal of being oneself and following one's own dream. And she has realized that her dream involves caring for dogs. A closely related theme is that sometimes it is necessary to disappoint parental expectations in order to fulfill one's dream. In Heidi's case, Leonard, her uneducated, intellectually starved father, wants her to be an intellectual. But Heidi spurns his vision when she meets Jane Anne Mosely, the avant-garde young writer from Greenwich Village for whom Leo sacrificed his marriage and family. She also rejects her mother's desire to make her glamorous so that she will attract a wealthy husband. Never again will she feel like a female impersonator as the result of a three-hour makeover at Elizabeth Arden's. After all, where had this glamour scheme got her mother? Petite, pretty Shirley had indeed married a wealthy man, but her large alimony payments fail to make her happy. Poor, homeless Jeffrey, on the other hand, possesses a hopeful philosophy Heidi can embrace.

In addition to the personal insights Heidi gains from knowing Jeffrey, he expands her external world by providing firsthand knowledge of the homeless. At her insistence, Jeffrey shows her the abandoned, boarded-up brownstone where he and four other people sleep. Even though Heidi has heard quite a bit about the homeless from television and newspapers, she is nevertheless shocked and dismayed by the squalor in which Jeffrey lives. The apartment floor is strewn with old mattresses, dirty blankets, candles in wine bottles, and piles of sundry possessions. The weather outside is freezing, and there is no water or electricity. Jeffrey and the other homeless people get food and baths at the various churches and shelters, but it is too dangerous to sleep there because people attack them. But Jeffrey does not sleep well even in the abandoned brownstone; it's too cold and he fears someone will steal his tape recorder. Seeing the world through Jeffrey's eyes, Heidi becomes conscious of the privileged life she leads and contemplates the profound unfairness of it all.

Heidi's relationship with Jeffrey also gives her a window into the life of a gay male. Because she feels comfortable with Jeffrey, Heidi asks him about being gay, and Wersba, once again, addresses the topic of sexual orientation. Heidi learns that Jeffrey has always known he is gay, and that being gay is not a choice but a simple fact. She knew he left Chicago because gangs there continually engaged in "gay bashing," but she learns firsthand what he is up against when he is accosted by two boys in Greenwich Village. In an unprecedented response, Jeffrey fights back and saves himself from a terrible beating. As he defends himself, Heidi observes that he really is "as male as the two kids who . . . tried to beat him up" (120). He does not have to act effeminately, but generally chooses to if he feels nervous or unsure of himself. When she meets his gay friends, Heidi realizes one cannot discern, from physical appearance, that a person is gay. In addition, she experiences an acute sense of separateness, as though the gay community is a club to which she will never belong. She must be who she is. Once again Jeffrey has, albeit inadvertently, assisted Heidi in developing her own individualism.

Wonderful Me

In *Wonderful Me* Heidi continues the nonviolent revolt against her parents that she began in *Just Be Gorgeous*. It is now summer, so the overcoat is no longer an issue, but Heidi continues to dress like a boy and keep her hair cut short. Shirley, who is now dating a podiatrist, has stopped nagging Heidi about her appearance, but when Leonard learns Heidi has decided not to attend college after graduation from prep school, he curtails her generous allowance. Whereas Heidi had previously considered various ways to earn a living, such as becoming a car shepherd, a massage therapist, or a veterinarian's assistant, she now takes a summer job as a professional dog walker. To Leonard's dismay, she earns 80 dollars a day by walking eight dogs simultaneously. Heidi is pleased because she is working with dogs and because she can take Happy to work with her—he makes the ninth dog on their jaunts through Central Park.

Because she still perceives herself as a short, plump, klutzy teenager with a voice that resembles Woody Allen's, Heidi is astounded to learn that her English teacher, the terrifically handsome but dull 23-year-old Lionel Moss, has left his position at

Spencer School because he is in love with her. Even though Shirley would be pleased by Lionel's physical attractiveness, Leonard would applaud his intellect, and even though Lionel, an avid walker, would help her walk the dogs, Heidi knows the relationship would be inappropriate. She tries to discourage Lionel but is amazed to discover he sees her as "a free spirit—young, fresh, witty, and filled with hope." In Lionel's eyes she is "charming and funny, and bright and original," and he tells her, "I think you are wonderful."[2] Jeffrey is the only other person who has ever told Heidi she is wonderful, and she is puzzled.

In addition to his flowery love letters, Lionel sends Heidi roses, takes her to romantic restaurants, and continually proclaims his devotion to her. When he places his mother's precious diamond-and-sapphire ring on her finger and tells her they are engaged, Heidi does not resist. In a daze she asks herself, "Who, besides Lionel, would ever find me attractive?" (107). Perhaps it doesn't matter if she does not share Lionel's feeling of romantic love. After all, where had love got her with Jeffrey? Deciding to make it a *long* engagement, but in the meantime not wanting to remain a virgin, Heidi plans to seduce Lionel when her mother is out of town. Her inept sexual advances fail, however, and Heidi learns Lionel does not believe in premarital sex. Although she is the woman he loves, he tells her they "must wait until marriage to consummate [their] passion"; anything less would "shock and dismay" him (120).

With the awkward question of sex out of the way for the time being, Heidi and Lionel become congenial companions. They visit his favorite store, the Urban Walker; dine in restaurants; buy books; walk the dogs; and read aloud the poetry of Rupert Brooke, the World War I English poet about whom Lionel is writing his master's thesis. When Heidi fears her mother may marry "El Creepo" (5), the podiatrist, she finds comfort in knowing she has Lionel. She talks to him about her loneliness, her decision not to attend college, her love for dogs, and he tries to understand. When she acquires another dog, an unwanted Scottie named Mac-Gregor, Lionel prepares a celebratory picnic in Central Park. He gives Happy and MacGregor each an expensive new leather collar and leash. This gesture touches Heidi so deeply that she falls in love with Lionel. After all, who else really understands her passion for dogs? Now Heidi feels truly attracted to Lionel. Lionel, in turn, responds to her physical overtures, and their relationship becomes intensely passionate, although unconsummated. The relationship ends abruptly, however, when Lionel's aunt Clemence, the woman who raised him, discovers Heidi in Lionel's apartment while he is at the dentist's. Heidi quickly learns, via the domineering Clemence Vale, that Lionel is quite mad and actually believes himself to be Rupert Brooke. He is supposed to be receiving psychiatric treatment from a doctor on Fifth Avenue but has not been keeping his appointments. Heidi also learns of the cruel upbringing Lionel has had with his aunt and her companion, Cornelia. But Heidi is shocked when Lionel returns and finds his aunt there; he immediately "changed into a little boy and Aunt Clemence changed into Florence Nightingale" (148). Realizing that Clemence Vale, who is a famed mystery writer, has created a true-life story of power and dependency, with Lionel as her central character, Heidi leaves the pathetic scene. Emotionally devastated and utterly confused about her sense of reality, Heidi realizes her first instinct had been accurate—he *was* psychotic. She is now able to understand that she did not love Lionel for anything about himself. She loved him for loving her.

Lionel Moss is one of Wersba's most bizarre, but fascinating, characters. The physical resemblance he bears to the poet may have intrigued Lionel when he was 14, but that Brooke was also raised by a domineering woman, in his case his mother, could conceivably have magnified Lionel's lingering identification with the young poet. It was not difficult for Lionel to imitate Brooke's mode of dress and affinity for physical exercise. And it follows suit that he, like Brooke, would love a female much younger than himself and who is overwhelmed by his affections. That Heidi and Lionel are parted before their love is consummated parallels what happened to Brooke and his young love when he was killed in the war. Lionel plays his part brilliantly and his character enables Wersba to add several literary layers to the novel.

The poetry Lionel quotes and the biographical information he imparts about writers and poets lend a literary ambience to *Wonderful Me* similar to that which Mrs. Woodfin, Chandler Brown, and Arnold Bromberg bring to earlier Wersba novels. Indeed, Lionel's enthusiasm for literature is so strong that Heidi, who previously disliked fiction, emerges from their baffling relationship with a genuine appreciation of literature. In addition, because Lionel's aunt is a writer, Wersba is able to comment on another literary genre, this time the gruesome mystery novels popular with many readers. But as she criticizes these thrillers, she also makes fun of her own novel when she has Heidi mentally tell Miss Vale, "[Y]ou've missed quite a plot here. It's even more colorful than that corpse you placed in the bottom of the aquarium" (151).

Strange as the story of Heidi and Lionel may be, *Wonderful Me* is often humorous. Lionel's love letters, although disconcerting to Heidi, are highly amusing, for example, as he tells her "you are as dear to me as a young foal gamboling in a meadow" (19) and "you are heaped clouds, tinged with the sunset" (52). Lionel's archaic way of speaking to her and the natural, unsophisticated, teenage voice in which Heidi responds also create humorous effects, as in this exchange that follows Heidi's failed seduction of Lionel:

> He smiled. "You are so adorable, and so very young. Whenever I look at you, my heart falters."
> "No kidding."
> "Yes," said Lionel, in his element again, "my heart falters with happiness, and I hear the song of a nightingale. In *that* way, little Heidi, do I love you." (121)

Heidi's reveries are also comical. After Lionel delivers the speech in which he insists upon waiting until marriage to have sex, Heidi is unable to respond because, as she puts it, "all I could see was an image of Lionel and me on our wedding night, trying to consummate our passion. We were lying in bed completely clothed, and he was reading Virginia Woolf" (120).

Wersba also has fun with human affectations. Mr. Balboa, the owner of the Urban Walker where Lionel buys his walking gear, is quite serious about his elaborate walking systems. He sells everything one needs for perambulation, such as walking suits, walking socks, walking hats, and walking underwear. When Heidi innocently asks why people need special clothes for walking, he explains that "they simply provide a little more style, a little more chic" (79). Heidi politely says she understands, but she really doesn't and the absurdity of the situation shines through. Even more ludicrous are the affectations people extend to their dogs. In earlier novels Wersba has poked fun at dog owners who purchase expensive raincoats for their canines, but some of the dogs Heidi walks even wear galoshes!

Shirley's misunderstandings provide amusement as well—Freud was some German man addicted to cocaine, T. S. Eliot wrote the musical *Cats*, Van Gogh tried to cut off his nose—but they also illustrate the communication problem between Heidi and her mother. When Heidi tells her mother she is having dinner with Claude Debussy, Shirley doesn't understand Heidi's joke and asks if Debussy is a foreign name. But lack of communication runs deeper than failed wisecracks. Heidi has never confided in her parents and believes few people tell their parents the truth. Even though her mother tells Heidi the problems she has with the podiatrist she is dating, and at one point Heidi yearns to tell Shirley all about Lionel and ask her advice, Heidi is unable to unburden herself to her mother. When Shirley stops dating the doctor, Heidi realizes her mother's attention will once again focus on her daughter's appearance. Heidi's decision not to attend college will also be discussed in a "family conference" (153), although Heidi does not expect any real communication to take place.

Peculiar as he was, at least Lionel was someone to talk to the summer Heidi turned 17, and although she never hears from him again after he sends her a farewell bouquet, her experience with him has made her more independent. Frustrated by romance, Heidi swears off men and confirms her desire to work with dogs. For like many of Wersba's characters, Heidi still likes animals more than people.

The Farewell Kid

In *The Farewell Kid*, Heidi, who is now almost 18, has graduated from Spencer School and is more determined than ever to dedicate her life to dogs. But she now feels called to devote herself to strays rather than "pampered pedigreed dogs."[3] Because she has decided, against her parents' wishes, not to attend college, she must support herself. While her mother is in Europe and her father is involved in a new love affair, Heidi rents a defunct barbershop in which she sets up housekeeping and starts Dog Rescue, Incorporated. Her motto is "If you lose a dog, we will find him. If you wish to adopt a dog, we will provide one" (50).

One rainy day, Heidi is unexpectedly assisted in rescuing her first stray, an Irish setter, by a boy named "Harvey Beaumont the Third." Harvey, from Wersba's *The Carnival in My Mind*, is quite experienced with Irish setters, thanks to his mother's expertise. Heidi later phones him and Harvey comes to the barbershop to help her control the new stray's maniacal behavior. Discovering they have much in common, Harvey and Heidi become friends. Together they enjoy visiting museums and photography shows (Harvey is now involved with photography rather than writing), walking Heidi's dogs in Central Park (she has four strays since taking in a 10-year-old Chihuahua), and going out to dinner. Harvey wants their relationship to advance, but Heidi is firm in her assertion that they remain just friends.

When he can no longer abide a platonic relationship, Harvey writes a letter, telling Heidi he thinks she is wonderful, but they must part. Heidi seeks comfort in her dogs, but after four lonely days, she goes to Harvey's Fifth Avenue apartment to discuss the situation with him. Expecting Holmes, the butler, to answer the door, Heidi instead encounters Harvey's mother, Muriel Beaumont. Muriel tells her, quite coldly, that Harvey is visiting his father in Connecticut, and she has no idea when he will return. Heidi senses that Muriel is strongly anti-Semitic.

Knowing Harvey runs daily at dawn, Heidi waits across the street from his apartment each day until he eventually returns to the city. The morning he finally appears, she chases him for 12 blocks, catching up when he stops to check his watch. Breathless, Heidi staggers up to him and, to her astonishment, through tears and kisses, tells him that she loves him.

Back at the barbershop, Harvey pales as Heidi describes her meeting with his mother. When Heidi tells Harvey she doesn't think he should be living with his mother, he asks her where he should live. "Here, with me," she quickly responds (137). Although they are both virgins, the time is right and they become lovers. Their new relationship is wonderful for them both. Harvey moves in with Heidi, and they make the necessary adjustments in their personal habits to allow for successful cohabitation. In addition to making a success of the dog rescue business, they each plan to pursue their educations. Harvey will enroll at Manhattan Institute of Photography and Heidi, to please her father, will take a few classes at Hunter College. Marriage is definitely in their future.

By uniting these two misfits, Wersba provides love, happiness, and a sense of human connection for both Heidi and Harvey. The match seems appropriate, for as Harvey observes, they are two of a kind. They are both loners who were outcasts in prep school and whose need for understanding and companionship has involved them in some rather odd relationships with older people. Both were unmotivated students but are highly self-motivated when it comes to pursuing their own interests. Neither plans a traditional college education. Although they are solitary people, they are kind, sympathetic, and capable of maintaining a loving relationship. In fact, their mutual understanding of the importance of solitude is one of their main strengths as a couple. In Rilke's words, they, as lovers, will be "guardians of each other's solitude" (qtd. 154). Heidi immediately begins to guard their privacy when she tells Shirley not to drop in on her anymore.

Both Heidi and Harvey come from wealthy families in which the parents are separated and in which child/parent relationships have been strained. However, they have achieved good relationships with their fathers, both of whom support Heidi and Harvey's decision to live together. Their mothers are more possessive and less accepting of the situation. Shirley will still probably try to run Heidi's life, but Heidi has learned how to deal with her gently but effectively; Muriel, although stunned by the situation, is powerless because Harvey came of age when she wasn't paying attention. But Heidi and Harvey understand enough about their mothers to accept them for who they are. Ironically, Heidi's encounter with Muriel enables Heidi to appreciate her own mother; for as eccentric and pushy as Shirley may be, at least she loves her daughter. Experiencing Muriel's unpleasantness helps Heidi understand Harvey's lack of confidence and his strong need for mothering.

Fortunately, Heidi and Harvey have gained enough self-knowledge to understand the importance of a balanced relationship. Harvey knows that being too needy is unattractive; Heidi realizes that "love [doesn't] have to be something you drown in" (154). Harvey is more than just a stray who needs her; he is her male counterpart, a kind and gentle lover, and her best friend. By intertwining the stories of two likable characters as they say farewell to adolescence and hello to independence, Wersba satisfies not only the lonely misfits Heidi and Harvey but her readers as well.

In this second trilogy, Wersba refines her skill at sequel writing. Whereas Rita Formica's story could probably have been condensed to one volume, the three parts of Heidi's story are all distinctly different and told with much less repetition. In *The Farewell Kid*, for example, most of the overlap, apart from the first few chapters, comes in the form of exposition as Heidi and Harvey get to know each other by becoming acquainted with each other's past. In addition to advancing plot and character development, these information exchanges serve as gentle reminders for readers familiar with Wersba's previous books, or as enticements for readers who have not read *Just Be Gorgeous* and *Wonderful Me* to read those books. Of course, only readers familiar with *The Carnival in My Mind* will know Harvey has already had his own Wersba book, and only these readers can share in the double pleasure brought by the conclusion of *The Farewell Kid* as Heidi and Harvey begin to march to drummers who perhaps play variations of the same theme.

Wersba intended Heidi's story to be a trilogy when she began writing it.[4] The idea for the first book came from something she heard Joan Rivers say on television. Wersba was working in the kitchen when she heard Rivers say, "Just be gorgeous." Wersba laughed at this, and the phrase eventually inspired her to create the characters of Heidi and Shirley Rosenbloom. Jeffrey Collins, in *Just Be Gorgeous*, like Chandler Brown, in *The Carnival in My*

Mind, is based on would-be performers Wersba knew in her acting days when she lived in Greenwich Village. Wersba has no idea where *Wonderful Me*'s Lionel Moss came from, but she had always worried about Harvey Beaumont the Third and was pleased to find him a home in *The Farewell Kid.*

As with most of Wersba's titles, critics spoke highly of the Heidi books. A few mentioned minor weaknesses in some plot details, but most praised the characterization throughout the trilogy as well as Wersba's delicate style, abundant compassion, and subtle humor. Hazel Rochman, in her *Booklist* review of *Just Be Gorgeous*, writes that "in usual Wersba style, the novel ends with a controlled sense of loss and renewal."[5] When reviewing *Just Be Gorgeous*, Joanne Aswell, of the *School Library Journal,* begins, "Wersba has again created one of her unlikely duos in another story of teenage disillusionment."[6] She, like many other reviewers of the trilogy, uses the phrase "Wersba fans," saying they will not be disappointed. These reviews make it clear that Barbara Wersba has garnered a dedicated readership, readers who do not necessarily demand she break any new ground, but who appreciate her fine writing, interesting characters, and intriguing stories. The Heidi stories do not always measure up to Wersba's previous works, in some reviewers' opinions, but few hesitate to recommend them. Indeed, *The Farewell Kid* was selected by ALA's Young Adults Services Department (YASD) for the 1991 Books for Reluctant Young Adult Readers list.[7] Like the Rita Formica books, all three of the Heidi Rosenbloom trilogy were published in paperback by Dell.

The trilogy begins with two unlikely relationships that do not last long but assist Heidi on her journey through adolescence. The third ends in a more permanent relationship. Two shorts and one long may signal distress for some, but for Heidi it means that she has learned enough about herself, her parents, and love to establish herself in an adult relationship. She still loves stray dogs, but she has moved beyond the canine world in her giving and receiving of affection. Three men have declared her wonderful, but it is her own determination to be herself and her compassion for others that makes her appealing (even gorgeous) to Wersba's readers.

6. Outrageous Adventures and Amazing Coincidences: *The Best Place to Live Is the Ceiling, You'll Never Guess the End,* and *Life Is What Happens While You're Making Other Plans*

Archie Smith, Joel Greenberg, and Justin Weinberg, three depressed young men, have some incredible experiences in *The Best Place to Live Is the Ceiling, You'll Never Guess the End,* and *Life Is What Happens While You're Making Other Plans*. As Wersba grows more playful with her novels, she writes spoofs in which Archie is involved with diamond smuggling in Zürich and Joel is part of a New York City kidnapping. Wersba turns more serious with Justin, who discovers that dreams can come true when he actually meets the New Zealand actress Kerry Brown.

The Best Place to Live Is the Ceiling

Highly intelligent social outcast Archie Smith, who is 16 but looks 19 and lives in Queens with his widower father, longs to escape his boring life and experience adventure. He dreams of traveling to a foreign land, of "shedding his life like a snakeskin, and starting

113

over."[1] His fantasies also involve romantic encounters with stars of old films, such as Elizabeth Taylor and Gloria Swanson; he "*live[s] for old movies*" (16–17). Archie's dreams *do not* include being his father's housekeeper. Obsessed with foreign travel, Archie collects travel brochures, frequents travel agencies, and keeps a dossier on world travel. He considers himself unattractive to the opposite sex and generally feels like "a very old man who bears a slight resemblance to Woody Allen" (8). When he is particularly depressed, he sits in the Skyview Restaurant at Kennedy Airport and imagines the places he could go if he were aboard a 747.

One evening he is sitting in the Skyview when a blond young man, Brian Chesterfield, who resembles Archie, joins him at his table. Brian, who is expensively dressed, wears a purse on a strap over his shoulder. Helping himself to a handful of peanuts, he tells Archie he is going on a skiing vacation in Switzerland. Suddenly, Brian takes a sip of his scotch, has an attack, and falls to the floor, unconscious. As two paramedics whisk him away on a stretcher, Archie notices the purse has been left behind. He picks it up and discovers Brian's plane ticket to Zürich, complete with boarding pass and baggage claim check, his passport, $2,000 in traveler's checks, $3,000 in American cash, a reservation confirmation from the Hotel Opera, and a small red address book. When Swissair flight 100 leaves for Zürich, Archie Smith, impersonating the presumed-dead Brian Chesterfield, is on the flight.

Archie does not know it, but Brian is the delivery boy for an international diamond-smuggling caper. Archie unwittingly follows the instructions of a man named Gessner and picks up some black sealskin boots at a local shop in Zürich. But by now a group of thugs is after him. Luckily Archie has hooked up with Polo Quinn, a very unusual 16-year-old American girl whose father, ironically, is a famous writer of suspense novels. Archie and Polo temporarily evade their pursuers by escaping to Davos, where Polo's father owns a villa, but Gessner and associates locate them and pressure them for "the goods" (113). Archie and Polo return to Zürich and hide among Polo's street-people friends.

In the course of their adventure Archie has fallen in love with Polo, and she finally lets down her emotional guard long enough to let him know she likes him as well. The impression she has given of having had many lovers is false. She, like Archie, is a virgin. They make love in Archie's sleeping bag, but their contentment is interrupted the next morning when the Zürich police make a routine sweep of teenagers sleeping in the park. Archie and Polo are taken to the police station, where Archie tells the officials he has entered the country illegally. The police escort him first to the train station to get his belongings from a locker and then to Kloten Airport. Archie notices Gessner and the others following him in the train station and angrily glares at them as the police put him on a plane for New York. He still does not know that the crepe soles of his sealskin boots are hollow and contain many small plastic bags filled with diamonds.

Archie's father is overjoyed to see him, but Archie is in trouble with the New York police. He turns Brian Chesterfield's possessions over to them, except for the address book and the fur boots. Archie is still trying to find out what Gessner and company were after. He locates Shirley Malone, Brian's old girlfriend, via Brian's address book. Shirley tells Archie that while Brian was hospitalized after having an allergic reaction to the combination of peanuts and scotch, he was arrested on charges of theft unrelated to the Zürich caper. Brian told her all about the diamond deal, hoping that she would contact Gessner, but she refused to become involved. She and Archie discover the diamonds hidden in the boots, 100 diamonds in all, and, wanting to rid themselves of the whole affair, hide them in an old hot-water bottle. They toss the hot-water bottle into the East River and watch it float out of their lives.

Archie misses Polo terribly. She understood his loneliness, had shared his adventure, and she was his first love. He tries to phone her in Davos, but the maid tells him Polo and her father are in Barcelona. It occurs to Archie that although he told Polo he loved her, she never said the same to him. He suspects he may never see her again, but he starts collecting travel brochures on Spain just in case. Archie is still a loner and probably always will be, but his outlook has changed for the better. He no longer agrees with the graffiti written on the cement wall near his high school that say "the best place to live is the ceiling" (8). He now believes "the best place to live is the world" with all its exciting possibilities (184). Archie's story is told through journal entries written to his psychologist, Dr. Gutman. The doctor will not be reading the notebook, but through it Archie reveals his feelings of loneliness, his thoughts of suicide, his dreams about older women, and his fear that all of his father's housekeeping demands will turn him into a transvestite. He describes the fantasies he has while Dr. Gutman talks during their sessions, fantasies about being a double agent, an Irish terrorist, a famous polo player, or a brilliant writer. In fact, when he begins to relate his Swiss adventure to Dr. Gutman in his journal, Archie writes: "It's so fantastic that it's like one of the scenarios I invent while you talk about the weather. But this time it is real, Dr. Gutman. Real, actually happening. And to me" (23).

Archie continues to record his bizarre experience in his notebook so that, as he says, Dr. Gutman can read it when Archie is in jail. Much of Archie's notebook chronicles the story of his fantastic adventure, but it also describes his impressions of the breathtaking Swiss Alps, the intriguing city of Zürich, and the interesting Swiss people. Archie concludes his journal by restating his dislike for therapy, but it is clear that keeping a journal has had a therapeutic effect on him. It has given him someone to confide in, and even though Dr. Gutman will never know about Archie's writing, Archie has indeed explored and improved his life.

One area of Archie's life that has improved is his relationship with his father. Roger Darlington Smith teaches children's literature at a small college. He has been writing his dissertation on P. L. Travers for 10 years. He calls Mary Poppins "the cosmic nanny" (5) and ponders the existential meaning of *Alice in Wonderland*. A cat lover, Mr. Smith constantly brings home strays and names them according to his passion in life: Lewis Carroll, Hans Christian, L. Frank Baum, J. M. Barrie, Newbery, Caldecott, the Brothers Grimm, Kipling, Tarkington, Thurber, and the Countess d'Aulnoy. Archie sees his father as a nice man, highly intellectual, but a loser because he is out of step with the world beyond academia. He embarrasses Archie because he is different from other fathers. While Archie is in Switzerland, however, he misses his father and yearns to share the beauty of the Alps with him. Even more important, he comes to appreciate his father by contrasting him with Polo's father.

Polo's father, Christopher Quinn, a famous writer of suspense novels, is also a widower. He has never paid much attention to Polo. In fact, Polo knows he never wanted a child in the first place. Finding her behavior incorrigible ever since her mother died, he has washed his hands of her. Polo is so starved for his attention that she smokes, swears, shoplifts, and lives with the street people in Zürich. She believes outrageous behavior is the only way to make her father notice her. As Polo puts it, "It's the only goddam communication we have" (99). Christopher Quinn's work clearly comes first in his life, followed by his love of fame and knowing important people.

Perceiving Polo's pain, Archie realizes that he, "at least, had been wanted" (103). Although his father "may never accomplish a thing in this world, he had always acted like [Archie was] a star" (103). Wersba may be using Roger Smith to poke a little fun at academics who overanalyze children's literature, but he is clearly a loving father. Mr. Smith blames himself for Archie's running away, but Archie knows his desire for adventure has nothing to do with parental inadequacy. He just yearns for the excitement of exotic places.

Polo's mother once cautioned her to "be careful what you wish for, because it just might happen" (106). Archie's wildest dreams certainly come true with his adventure in Switzerland. Polo, on the other hand, just wants a normal life. In an uncharacteristically intimate conversation with Archie, she confides: "I wish I could come back to America with you. And go to your crummy high school, and take exams, and date, and just be a normal person. I'm so tired of being me" (115). But poor-little-rich-girl Polo has less chance of living a normal life than Archie did of falling in with diamond smugglers. Obsessed by fame and fortune, her father moves her around the world as he explores the settings for his thrillers. Polo's wishes do not matter at all.

The Best Place to Live Is the Ceiling parodies the popular adventure/suspense/thriller novels that Christopher Quinn writes. Quinn's books, of which Archie has read many, are filled with spies, intrigue, and lost, beautiful women (68). So of course Archie's adventure is filled with chase scenes through the streets of Zürich, daring jumps out of second-story windows, long train rides to Swiss villages, speedy exits from restaurants to avoid pursuit, bodyguards, death threats, police escorts, international diamond smugglers, and one elaborate hoax after another. Polo becomes a key player, devising schemes to confront and evade the gangsters, showing herself to be brave and imaginative, just as Archie is discovering himself to be. In the midst of their escapades Polo observes, "We should really give this whole situation to my father. He could use it as a thriller" (99). Hearing about Archie's adventure, Shirley Malone, Brian Chesterfield's ex-girlfriend and an unemployed actress, believes the story would make a great play. She comments, "[W]hat a scenario. Put it in a play and no one would believe it" (177).

Implausible, yes; but fun to read, definitely. Wersba's fast-paced tale is so far-fetched that one has to laugh out loud. In addition, Wersba infuses humor into the narrative with entries like this from a perplexed Archie:

> *March 8* Dr. Gutman, I keep asking myself, if I had this whole thing to do over again, would I? Because I am now a hunted man, a fugitive, and that was not exactly my purpose in coming to Europe.
>
> I am so angry at B.C. that I could kill him. I don't care if he *is* lying in a hospital somewhere, paralyzed, worrying about his luggage and his black purse. He should never have got me into this mess. (72)

The contrast between the speech of tough-talking Polo and prim-sounding Archie is also amusing. Polo tells Archie he talks "like a faggot" (69); Archie writes Dr. Gutman that "every time she says fuck I want to wash her mouth out with soap" (101). Easily shocked, Archie is the perfect straight man for the irrepressible Polo Quinn.

On the aesthetic side, the book is also a travelogue, featuring Zürich and Davos and starring the Swiss Alps. With a new friend called Mrs. Mendelsohn as guide, Archie and the reader are treated to a tour of Zürich. She tells us: "This side of the river is called the Limmatquai, and soon we will pass the historic Water Chapel. On the other side, you can see the spires of Fraumunster and St. Peter's. . . . Those are the old guild halls. . . . And there, on your left, is Grossmunster, the famous cathedral. The river you are admiring opens out to the Zurichsee, Lake Zurich, and beyond, of course, are the Alps" (38). Archie continues the tour as he strikes out on his own in Zürich and then with Polo in Davos and the Alps. The descriptions create vivid images of these places, the scenery, and the general ambience. Those familiar with Zürich and the Alps will appreciate the accuracy of the verbal portraits; those inspired to visit will find themselves equipped with a prose map adequate for assisting travel plans. The freshness with which Archie expresses his awe at all he sees, his sometimes off-the-wall explanations, and his careful attention to detail make his travel commentary pleasing reading.

Wersba wrote this extended self-analysis of a lonely teenager—a spoof of the suspense novel and a travelogue merged into one month's journal entries—as a tribute to her joyful visits to Switzerland with her friend Zue. She was also deeply immersed in reading James Bond books and thought "wouldn't it be fun to have a junior James Bond."[2] At one time she thought of taking Archie on adventures all over the world, rather like a "baby James Bond," but after Zue's death Wersba lost her enthusiasm for this idea.

Archie's acquaintance with Melina Mendelsohn derives from an experience Wersba and Zue had with Mrs. Irwin Shaw. They were sitting on a plane almost ready to take off from Kennedy Airport when a well-dressed woman came rushing down the aisle, sat down in the seat next to Wersba, and stuffed her fur coat under her seat. Over the course of the flight the three of them became friendly, and on subsequent journeys to Switzerland, Wersba and Zue were houseguests in the Shaws' Klosters vacation home. This chance meeting led to a film version of *Carnival,* as is noted in chapter 1. Perhaps Archie's meeting Polo and going to her father's home in the Alps may not be the outrageous coincidence one might imagine it to be.

Critics held varying views of *Ceiling*. Most agreed that it was a fast-paced adventure with beautiful descriptions of the Alps, but those who failed to see it as a "tongue-in-cheek thriller,"[3] missed the point. As Trev Jones put it in the *School Library Journal*, "Those who take it all seriously will find several flaws; those who take it as intended—delightfully improbable and hilariously implausible—are in for a high-spirited romp through the Alps with a Woody Allen sound-alike."[4] Zena Sutherland in the *Bulletin of the Center for Children's Books* agreed, saying: "If this were serious, it would be ridiculous—but it isn't, it's a spoof, and one that is fast and funny."[5] As usual, reviewers commented positively on Wersba's characters. Susan Jelcich of *VOYA* wanted more Polo,[6] but *Publishers Weekly* summed up the characters aptly, saying "their authenticity makes this madcap tale seem nearly plausible" (Roback & Donahue, 128).

You'll Never Guess the End

Joel Greenberg, the hero of *You'll Never Guess the End*, is having a quiet nervous breakdown, not because he is jealous of his older brother's success, but because life seems so unfair. His brother JJ, who has written a best-seller called *Stirring Constantly*, is hailed by *Manhattan* magazine as the J. D. Salinger of the 1990s, frequently interviewed on television shows, and forgiven by his and JJ's parents for his recent crimes. Previous to writing the book, JJ had been arrested for dealing cocaine; had dropped out of Columbia University; and returned home to Fifth Avenue to live with his family, performing community service instead of going to jail. Then he wrote *Stirring Constantly*, on a bet from a friend, and became a 20-year-old celebrity overnight. The injustice, according to Joel, who used to admire his brother, is that the book, "a long, boring monologue delivered by a temporary typist named Merry Graves,"[7] isn't even any good. Joel, who was 15 when all this happened, continued getting good grades at Lincoln School, walking his dog, Sherlock, doing errands for his mother, and feeding the homeless in Central Park. He is reliable, but he wants to be recognized as someone special and unusual. JJ, however, is filling that role in their family; Joel is being ignored.

Then Marilyn Schumacher, JJ's ex-girlfriend, is kidnapped and her father, a multimillionaire business tycoon, refuses to pay the ransom. Mr. Schumacher fears the $100,000 is really blackmail for defense secrets he cannot divulge. Joel had always liked Marilyn because, even though she is not too bright and shopping is her raison d'être, she is a kind person. He, along with several others, wants to solve the mystery. Hannah, the Greenberg's maid, tells her Scientific Religion group to concentrate positive thoughts in Marilyn's direction. Joel's mother, Buffy, and her Ladies' Discussion Group hire a psychic, who sends them on a wild goose chase to a fish restaurant in Sag Harbor. JJ acts unconcerned, but he secretly arranges for an actor-friend of his own to help search for Marilyn. Two more of Marilyn's ex-boyfriends hire a private detective. Joel consults his homeless friend Solo Jones, who claims to have been a police detective at one point, and decides to use his dog, Sherlock, who is part bloodhound, to find Marilyn.

Sherlock eventually leads Joel to Marilyn, who is being held captive in a shabby hotel on West 14th Street. Marilyn, it turns out, has arranged for her dry cleaners, Solly and his brother Mike, to kidnap her so she could repay a $50,000 bridge debt. She has promised the other $50,000 of the ransom money to the brothers, whose dry-cleaning shop had recently suffered fire damage. They are all baffled because Marilyn's father is taking so long with the ransom. Marilyn would like to call it quits, but the others want the money. Joel and Sherlock are captives until Joel saves the day by attaching a note to Sherlock's collar, lowering him from the third-story hotel window in a bedsheet sling, and commanding him to go home. JJ, Joel's father, two policemen, and Mr. Schumacher arrive soon after. They have Joel's note, but Sherlock has not nosed his way through the streets of New York to 82nd Street; someone read his identification collar and sent him home in a taxi.

Marilyn refuses to press charges against Solly and Mike because she has grown fond of them. She discovers the bridge debt was not intended to be taken seriously, but her father insists she give up the game anyway. She and JJ get back together, but each agrees to make some changes. Marilyn will seek professional help concerning her need to seduce men; JJ will take writing courses at the New School to learn the basics of writing. Joel realizes JJ actually does love Marilyn and that for all his bravado, he really does not think he writes well. Hannah applauds the good thoughts that led to Joel's deeds and tells him that if he keeps them up, he will really be somebody someday. Joel's parents praise him highly for his heroic actions, but he doesn't need their recognition so badly anymore.

Wersba has written another spoof. This time she parodies the mystery/detective genre. In addition to the implausible plot, all the speculation that takes place among the characters comments on the extreme situations inherent in the genre. When Marilyn is kidnapped, everyone has theories about what has happened to her: she is dead, dismembered, and strewn throughout the city; she has been sold into white slavery; she has been forced to change her identity; she has been abducted to Paris. The suspects abound: JJ kidnapped her himself; Ashley Brooks, Marilyn's ex-boyfriend three-times removed, spirited her away because he still loves her. Various reasons for Mr. Schumacher's refusal to pay the ransom arise: he is involved with the Mafia; he is afraid to risk a congressional investigation into his financial empire. Much of the speculation is based on mystery/detective films the characters have watched, but some of the scheme itself comes from these movies. When kidnappers Solly and Mike instruct Dan Schumacher to leave the ransom money in a train-station locker, they are following procedures learned from a Jimmy Cagney film. Although they don't say so, Joel and Marilyn could well have got the idea for the bedsheet rope from a detective movie, although using it to lower a lethargic bloodhound was Wersba's own comic touch.

Wersba also makes fun of a type of contemporary adult literature, which she calls "Yuppie Lit" (14), with an excerpt from JJ's novel *Stirring Constantly*:

> So I'm like, trying to take a nap on the Fifth Avenue bus, on my way to work, right?, when this dude sits down next to me and

begins to give me the eye. Fine, OK, I can deal with that, and anyway I'm trying to sleep for God's sake, but the dude just won't take his eyes off me. I mean, like, I have been out till four in the morning and now it is *eight* in the morning, and I am not a cheerful unit. (4–5)

JJ's novel ends when the narrator, Merry Graves, is sent to a rehab center where she manages to buy cocaine from one of the nurses. In his second novel, *Call It Black*, JJ hopes to launch a new genre called the "downtown novel," which captures the ambience of the city and in which the subtext is real estate (35–36).

You'll Never Guess the End—an ironic title because one knows from the beginning that Joel will save Marilyn and become the hero he needs to be—is filled with zany humor. The plot consists of one mishap after another, the biggest one being the failed ransom collection scheme, but much of the dialogue is also humorous. For example, Solo Jones, the homeless man in Central Park, chides Joel for not always bringing him the best sandwiches available in New York's delis. He also chastises Joel for not realizing that as a bloodhound, Sherlock is the key to the kidnapping mystery: "How come you never thought of that, Joel? Are you a moron?" (42). When Joel buys a book on training bloodhounds, he tells Sherlock, "You need to read this book" so that he'll know what he was born to do.

This is another fast-paced, fun-filled novel with a satisfying ending. But in addition to conducting a hilarious search throughout New York City, Joel grows personally; his relationships within his family improve, and he helps Marilyn find something other than shopping, bridge, and sex to fill her life. She now helps him hand out food to the homeless and is considering volunteering at a home for runaway kids. The somber side of life lingers, however, even through the laughter the novel elicits.

Reviewers unanimously praised *You'll Never Guess* for its humor and action, hailing it as a lighthearted mystery younger teens would find greatly entertaining. *Publishers Weekly* mentions Wersba's "satiric wit" and Joel's "gently mocking point of view."[8] Janice Del Negro of *Booklist* mentions the effectiveness of the "Keystone Cops humor thrown in for laughs," along with the book's suspense-thriller appeal, but doubts if the New York in-jokes will have meaning for junior-high readers.[9] *Kirkus* also mentions these in-jokes, and enlightens literary/New York out-siders through the following review:

> Wersba, who usually takes on teenage angst with a fair blend of honesty and high comedy, nearly steals her own show with a subplot that spoofs the "literati" of the adult book world. Joel's older brother, JJ Greenberg, has achieved Jay McInerney-like fame with his first book and is making the rounds of talk shows with other writers, like Jennie Tamowitz (from whom he seems to have borrowed some very *Slaves of New York*-style observa-tions). Joel suffers through the (he believes) unearned admira-tion—at least until JJ's ex-girlfriend, daughter of a Trump-like real estate tycoon, is kidnapped. . . . Light on plot, heavy on humor and dramatics, and likely to please Wersba's fans every-where—especially those who have access to the "inside" jokes.[10]

As for Wersba, she is not quite sure where the novel came from, but she knows the impatience she feels when reading best-selling authors whom she considers undeserving of recognition.

Life Is What Happens
While You're Making Other Plans

Justin Weinberg, 17 years old and just about to graduate from prep school, does not like the future his father has planned for him. George Weinberg, a successful periodontist, expects that Justin will go to college and medical school, then establish a med-ical practice and settle down on Long Island—just as he did. Justin's mother died two years ago, and Justin and his father con-tinue to live in the Hamptons in a huge converted barn on an acre of ground with a swimming pool in the affluent village of Water Mill. Ever since he was five, Justin has wanted to be an actor, but only his best friend and fellow-oddball Bruno Kaufmann knows about his dream. The time has come to tell his father he wants to go to acting school, not college, but Justin lacks the courage to do so. Depressed, almost suicidal, he watches *Dark Rider*, starring a new film actress, Kerry Brown, from New Zealand. Justin is immediately smitten with her beauty and overwhelmed by her brilliant acting. He not only loves her, but somehow feels fundamentally connected to her.

Bruno is surprised when Justin tells him about his deep attraction to Kerry Brown because Justin, believing himself to be short, weird, and unattractive, has resisted going out with girls. Bruno conducts research on Kerry Brown and gives Justin a magazine article about her and a guidebook to New Zealand. Justin writes to Kerry in care of the New Zealand Film Board, but this does not satisfy Bruno, who encourages him to visit Kerry in New Zealand. Justin decides to do this when his father will be away for eight days. His only problem is the $2,000 needed for the plane ticket. Bruno, who is a deeply depressed person, raises the cash by selling his stereo system before attempting his own suicide.

Bruno's suicide attempt fails, but he will not allow Justin to buy the equipment back. Bruno wants Justin to use the money for the trip. Justin makes the necessary travel arrangements, forges a note from his father excusing him from school, gives the housekeeper the week off, locates Kerry Brown's phone number, and calls to tell her he is on his way to New Zealand in hopes of visiting her. Kerry's cousin Fiona answers the telephone. In the course of a brief, but kind, conversation, Justin learns that Kerry Brown is not at home in Wanganui, New Zealand. She is visiting a film director named Martin Wellman in America. In fact, she is at Wellman's beach house in Southampton, on Long Island. Fiona gives Justin the phone number there, encouraging him to "give Kerry a ring in Southampton."[11] Justin is stunned. Kerry Brown is just four miles away. Bruno gets a tremendous laugh out of this amazing coincidence.

After Bruno helps him gather his nerve, Justin buys two dozen sweetheart roses and delivers them to Kerry Brown at Wellman's beach house. The maid asks who they are from, thanks Justin, and closes the door. Severely disappointed, Justin spends the day canceling his travel arrangements for New Zealand but returns to the Wellman estate in the evening. Depressed, he is moping around when Kerry leaves the house and walks out to the beach. Justin follows her. Knowing she is being trailed, Kerry turns and speaks to Justin. He identifies himself as the fan who sent the roses and, haltingly, tells her of his aborted plans to fly to New Zealand to visit her. Astonished, Kerry invites him back to the house for a drink. As Justin is leaving, he asks her advice about his becoming an actor. She agrees to view his video of himself doing Hamlet, and the next day tells him he has a "certain quality that's very good" (85) and that if he really wants to act, he should go directly to acting school, despite his father. Then she goes off to London with her fiancé, but writes Justin an encouraging note that makes him realize he is not as alone as he thinks.

Justin approaches his aunt Theo, an artist living in Manhattan's SoHo. She agrees to let him live with her while he attends acting school if he talks to his father first. She assures Justin his father loves him deeply, explaining that Justin causes him pain because he resembles his mother, whom his father adored. George was suicidal after her death until he went to therapy. Justin's father had wanted to be a shipbuilder, but his own father had insisted he attend dental school. Justin and Theo agree it's absurd the way history repeats itself in families. As Justin expected, George loses his temper when he tells him he wants to attend acting school instead of college. He calls acting a "fag profession" (110) and demands that Justin go to Barton College. Justin threatens to run away if forced to attend college. When George informs Justin he doesn't know what he is talking about, Justin says he hates him.

Justin decides to leave home for a few days until he can determine what to do. The Wellman estate is closed up, so Justin sleeps on the terrace. That night he senses a close, almost psychic connection to Kerry. In the morning Bruno, who intuits just where to find him, tells Justin his father is quite worried. Aunt Theo has come from SoHo, and they assume Justin has run away. When Justin returns home later that afternoon, he finds that Aunt Theo has talked with George, gently reminding him of some of the things his own father, a tyrannical, self-made man, did to him. Justin resolves to try to understand his father, not just complain about him. George decides to let Justin try acting school for the summer, but he hopes he will come home on weekends. Surprised to learn that his father will miss him, Justin promises to return to Water Mill every weekend.

The relationship between Justin and his father, George, is reminiscent of the relationship between David Marks and his father, Leo, in *Run Softly, Go Fast*. Both fathers are heavily engrossed in the self-made-man syndrome; both discount their sons' artistic dreams as being effeminate; and both use authoritarian tactics to try to control their offspring. Both sons fear their fathers and even tell them they hate them. However, Justin and George are able to resolve their differences in a way David and Leo never could, because the situation is much more intense in the case of the Marks family, with each side stubbornly holding its ground. Mrs. Marks tries to negotiate reconciliation, but her allegiance is more strongly tipped toward her husband, particularly when he is on his deathbed.

George Weinberg, however, who has already lost his wife, fears losing his son as well. In addition, his sister-in-law, Theo, has already absorbed much of his venom against "hippie" artists (103) as she struggled to become the successful painter she now is. Therefore, George is primed for Theo's gentle reminder about how his own father thwarted his youthful desire to become a shipbuilder. He is also able to accept her advocacy of Justin's desire to pursue an acting career.

Justin also has some mitigating experiences that make him want to understand his father. Aunt Theo helps when she discusses George's problems with Justin. But perhaps more importantly, Justin has seen Bruno struggle in his relationship with *his* father. So when Bruno recommends Justin not argue with his father, adding, as did Kerry Brown, that Justin is ultimately in charge of his own life, Justin takes his advice. Support from his aunt and best friend enable Justin to stop seeing his father as "a villain" (118) and meet him halfway: he assures his father he will not desert him, physically or psychologically.

The friendship between Bruno and Justin is mutually supportive. Justin shares his problems and fantasies with Bruno but knows there is a dark, depressed streak in his friend and does not press him to discuss certain topics. When Bruno finally talks about his suicide attempt, he explains that he thought he was a cipher whose life had no meaning, who could "*evaporate* and it still wouldn't make any difference" (68). Justin responds fiercely, saying, "That's a bunch of crap! You are the most valuable person I've ever known—and if you had succeeded in that garage, my whole life would have been ruined. Do you understand, Bruno?" (68–69). Justin's outburst registers with Bruno. At the end of the novel Bruno confesses that the infamous Bernie Glass, his adventurous friend who served as a model for them both as they plotted Justin's course of action, is only an imaginary friend, a prop Bruno made up but no longer needs. Ironically, Bruno's own life, the way he pulls himself together and, with the help of his psychiatrist, begins working toward a personal goal becomes an inspiration in and of itself.

Aside from some of Bruno's witty quips, humor is scarce in this novel. Instead, the natural landscape of the Hamptons provides an uplifting effect as Justin integrates his observations about the world of nature into his story. But rather than interpret his experiences in the manner of Archie Smith in *The Best Place,* Wersba allows them to form a backdrop of beauty, inspiration, and hope, subtly reminding us that nature holds the power to help human beings transcend their problems. Life, even if it is what happens while you're making other plans—as George, Bruno, and Justin join Heidi from *The Farewell Kid* in discovering—has a way of making things work out. Justin, like Wersba's many other protagonists, will be all right.

Life Is What Happens came out of Wersba's friendship with New Zealand writer Janet Frame, whom she had contacted by phone after being deeply moved by Frame's autobiography. Wersba and Frame carried on a telephone friendship for several years and they hoped to meet when Frame visited the States as part of a literary tour. However, when Frame arrived in Los Angeles, she was so disoriented that she never left the airport hotel. She returned to New Zealand after a few days. Both Frame and Wersba were disappointed that they did not meet as planned, but since Wersba was able to control Justin's life in a way she could not control her own, Justin's dream *could* be fulfilled.

Life Is What Happens While You're Making Other Plans was published in England where the *Junior Bookshelf* described it as "an amusing and touching book about the first moves away from school towards training and work" that will appeal to teens with a serious interest in film or who face an unpopular career choice.[12] Reconciliation with parents, particularly fathers, unites this chapter's three novels as Wersba continues to explore various ways that parents and their children can work though their differences and develop mutual understanding and respect. Maturation is a balance between lessening one's dependence on others for recognition and learning to rely upon oneself more fully, as Joel Greenberg accomplishes, and developing compassion for a parent's need for understanding, as Justin Weinberg does. Growing up also entails realizing, as Archie Smith does, how deeply a child can hurt a parent. Maturation is a lifelong journey; these three young men and their parents have helped each other travel great distances.

7. Seeking Solace: *Whistle Me Home*

At the beginning of her junior year at Sag Harbor's Peterson High, Noelle (Noli) Brown falls in love with new student Thomas Jerome (TJ) Baker when he reads a poem by Gerard Manley Hopkins to their English class. To Noli's amazement, TJ, who resembles a Greek god, singles her out to be his special friend. His sensitivity, curly brown hair, gold earring, and deeply tanned, athletic body have a dizzying effect on her. Unlike Noli's mother, TJ does not find Noli's appearance distasteful. In fact, he thinks her unevenly cropped red hair, jeans, hiking boots, and baseball cap make her look like a "beautiful tomboy."[1]

Stunned by the prospect of a future with TJ, Noli promises God that if He lets her have TJ, she will cut down on her drinking, try to get along with her mother, and stop shoplifting. It's a good time to be making this promise because the fights with her mother have become dangerous. In their last one, Noli had responded to Sally Brown's question, "When are you ever going to wear a dress?" by replying, "To your funeral" (23). Slapped across the face by her mother, Noli walks out and does not return until late that night. The two of them do not speak to each other for several days. In contrast to her mother, TJ shows Noli understanding; his caring, she believes, saves her life.

But Noli feels inadequate compared to TJ. He is a graceful, daring athlete; he writes brilliant essays; he reads poetry for pleasure; he sings sweetly and whistles beautifully. He has acted in an off-Broadway play and traveled in France. Although he used to drink himself senseless and smoke marijuana, he now abstains

130

from alcohol and drugs. TJ disapproves of Noli's drinking, but she needs liquor to calm her apprehensions about their relationship, just as she needs alcohol to suppress the rage she feels toward her mother. However, she quickly becomes a vegetarian so that their eating habits coincide, and tries to please him by not using four-letter words. When TJ says he loves her, her world brightens markedly.

Early in their relationship, TJ responds sympathetically when Noli tells him her mother had Alice, their miniature poodle, put to sleep because she had cancer. TJ promises to buy Noli another dog when the time is right. Later, wanting TJ to know the fears that lie behind the confident mask she wears for the rest of the world, Noli confides that a teenage boy sexually molested her when she was a child. TJ's response disappoints her. Although he understands that the experience still disturbs her, he tells her she must let go of it, turn it over to God, and stop acting like a victim. People, he says, must take responsibility for their lives. Noli decides she needs to know TJ better in order to understand his answer. She does not tell him of her recurring dream in which she is lost in New York City and can find no way to get home to Sag Harbor.

As they spend time together, Noli and TJ discover they share many interests in addition to an interest in old films. They enjoy browsing in junk stores, going to flea markets, walking on the beach, and riding TJ's motorbike. Noli has become interested in old books and peruses the secondhand bookstores with TJ. TJ gives her a striped pullover like his, and they buy white baseball caps, which they wear backwards. Almost like twins, both in their dress and their pursuits, they are together constantly.

But when Noli suggests that they cross-dress for the Halloween dance—he as Ingrid Bergman and she as Humphrey Bogart from *Casablanca*—TJ becomes enraged. Noli experiences TJ's anger again when she takes a drink before he comes to dinner with her parents. She also sees him throw another student against the lockers because of something he said about TJ's earring. Realizing TJ is not perfect, as she had once believed, but is "battling demons" (48) of some sort, Noli's love for TJ deepens.

In fact, she loves him so profoundly that she is eager to lose her virginity with him.

However, TJ still continues to kiss her gently, not passionately, and never becomes sexually aroused. He is a paradox to her. How can he be so sensitive and yet have such anger inside? How can he say he loves her but not desire her physically? She wonders if he is planning to become a priest, like Gerard Manley Hopkins. Ironically, Noli and her mother have a tremendous fight over whether or not Noli is having sex with TJ. Now TJ has entered her recurring dream; he is somewhere in New York City and she knows he would get her home to Sag Harbor if she could just find him, but she can't.

On Christmas morning, which is also her birthday, TJ brings Noli a new puppy, Alice the Second. Later, as they walk in the local cemetery, he confides in her for the first time by telling her about his grandmother. His grandmother, Caroline Ross, had great faith in him, believing he could be anything he wanted to be. When TJ expresses this kind of faith in Noli, she feels connected to the universe in a way she has never experienced before. She knows she will love TJ forever.

They celebrate New Year's Day by going into New York City. Although Noli now wants to wear feminine clothing for TJ, he continues to insist they dress as twins. So they both wear stonewashed jeans, boots, heavy jackets, and wool caps. Noli convinces TJ that they should take a cab to Greenwich Village, where a Dietrich double feature is showing. After the film, a young man with bleached-blond hair, who is dressed in men's clothing but wears women's high heels, rhinestone earrings, and eyeshadow, acts as though he knows TJ. TJ is rude to him and when he refers to Noli as a "trick" (62), TJ punches him. TJ and Noli run through the Village and finally stop at a coffee shop. TJ tells Noli the guy is a drag queen. There are lots of freaks in the Village, he explains, which is why he hesitated to take her there. Because his father is a writer and their family used to live in the Village, many people in the neighborhood know TJ. He is clearly upset, and so is Noli, partially because the drag queen thought she was a boy. She is relieved to be heading home to Sag Harbor on the luxurious Jitney bus, with TJ sleeping soundly, his head on her shoulder.

Noli and TJ continue to spend time together, but she is painfully aware that their relationship is not romantic. They hold hands at school and walk with their arms around each other, but they are friends rather than lovers. Still waiting for things to change, Noli begins to wonder what is wrong, either with TJ, or with her, or with them both. Alice the Second has entered into her recurring dream now. Noli tries desperately to find Alice in the labyrinth of New York City, so she can bring her dog back to Sag Harbor. Noli wakes, crying out, "I want to go home!" (68).

Knowing she already has a home, she wonders if her dream is a death wish. Finally she sees it as a cry for the safety she lacks. As she puts it, "Safety would be TJ's arms around her. Safety would be her and TJ in a warm bed, learning to make love" (68). Seeking comfort she cannot find with TJ, Noli continues to drink. Vodka "eases the tension. And she likes the way it feels going down her throat into her belly. Warm and all-pervading, like an embrace" (68).

In March her parents leave Noli alone in the house when they go away. Thinking it's now or never, if she and TJ are to become lovers, she invites him over. After eating dinner and watching a film on TV, TJ wants a drink. Noli, he points out, has already been drinking, and he decides to join her. They each have two glasses of vodka. TJ tries to make love to her, but he can't. As they lie naked on the rug in front of the fireplace, Noli asks TJ if he is gay and he bursts into tears. Noli wants to be understanding, but when TJ will not tell her about the kind of sex he engages in with other males, she becomes angry. Believing he chose her as a "cure" (74) because she looked like a boy, she refuses to listen to his declaration of love. She becomes verbally belligerent, calling TJ a "dirty faggot" and a "rotten queer" (74). When he leaves, Noli wants nothing more to do with him.

Utterly devastated, Noli gives herself a crew cut and increases her alcohol consumption. She is out of control and in trouble everywhere. When she comes to school drunk, the school psychologist recommends a teenage AA group; she refuses to attend any meetings until he tells her she will be suspended if she does not. Spurning her parents' attempts to reason with her, Noli steals money from her mother's purse and hocks her CD player in order to buy alcohol.

Learning that TJ has a new friend, an East Hampton preppie named Walker Lewis, Noli begins to spy on them. When she sees them together, dressed alike and laughing, it is clear to her that TJ has found a new twin. She senses that despite their macho appearance, they are lovers and share secrets she will never know. She is filled with regret for denying TJ the compassion and acceptance that would have allowed them to remain friends. However, when TJ sends her an Easter bouquet with a note saying he misses her, she is angry and confused. Believing she wants nothing from TJ, Noli leaves the flowers next door and takes Alice for a walk in the cemetery. After several drinks of vodka from her flask, Noli takes off Alice's collar and leash so she can chase squirrels among the tombstones. Absorbed in drunken daydreams, Noli does not watch Alice; and when she calls for her, she is gone.

Sick with the knowledge that drinking made her lose her beloved puppy, Noli promises God that if Alice returns, she will give up alcohol. When Melissa, Noli's new friend in AA, suggests she doesn't have to wait until Alice returns to stop drinking, Noli decides to try. Without liquor, her life is emptier than ever, so she adds two more AA meetings a week to fill the void. It is difficult, but Noli manages to stay sober. Melissa becomes her sponsor and helps her "take it a day at a time" (93).

Both Alice and TJ are now in Noli's dream about being lost in New York City. They are all three searching for each other, but none of them connect; as usual, no one in the city will help her get home. Somehow the dream is allowing her to work out her feelings about TJ. She realizes she no longer hates him, but she is confused by the idea of being friends with TJ and Walker. Their sexuality still troubles her, but she understands that TJ is seeking comfort in his own way, fighting his demons while trying to remain socially acceptable.

Suddenly, Alice is returned to Noli by a family who had taken her in. Touched by her mother's tears over Alice's return, Noli starts to "make amends" (97) for her formerly cruel behavior toward her. She now sees her mother as "just another suffering human being" (97). Later, she writes her mother a letter, apologizing for their quarrels and telling her she loves her.

When she bumps into TJ in early August on a Sag Harbor street, he tells her he misses her and is hurt by the things she said that night. Noli apologizes for her hurtful words but refuses to be friends. She is still emotionally and sexually attracted to TJ and does not want to settle for being the "female buddy of two gay boys" (104). Somehow she realizes that to acquiesce would be to lose herself and her potential for becoming her own person. Noli follows her instinct and makes a complete break with TJ; otherwise, "he will always be her prison, a beautiful box in which she is trapped." She must "be free of him so she can find herself" (105).

When her dream recurs that night, neither TJ nor Alice is in it. She is alone in New York without money and cannot even remember her phone number. Certain she will die of fear, she hears herself say, "Please. . . . Somebody help me! I need to go home" (107). And this time the dream allows her to go home to Sag Harbor. As she rides a supermodern bus speeding toward the east end of Long Island, she is filled with joy to be coming home to a life filled with possibilities. Sag Harbor itself offers her the solace she sought in liquor and an unsatisfying relationship. Sag Harbor will help her find herself. Sag Harbor, she realizes, *is* home. Noli has found her way home.

Whistle Me Home is essentially the same story about a misfit coming to terms with herself that Wersba relates in her other novels, but she takes several stylistic departures in this work. The most noticeable difference is the close third-person point of view rather than the first-person voice of her other protagonists. This shift in perspective allows Wersba to go beyond the main character's actual words and thoughts toward descriptions and ideas the protagonist might perceive but be unable to articulate. Thus Wersba does not have to make Noli an unusually intelligent or sensitive teen in order for her story to be told in a compelling fashion. The third person works well for Wersba, enabling her to recapture some of the intensity of her earlier writing.

In addition to, or perhaps because of, the freshness of the new voice used in *Whistle*, Wersba takes a deeper look at the topic of alcoholism. This subject is not new to Wersba, but by making Noli herself the alcoholic, rather than one of the secondary characters, Wersba is able to detail Noli's experiences as she seeks comfort in alcohol and then works to become sober. Now Wersba takes readers into AA meetings and allows them to listen to conversations among alcoholics at various points in the recovery process.

Wersba also addresses the topic of sexual orientation somewhat differently in *Whistle Me Home*. This time the protagonist is involved with a gay male in a way that provides insight into both the nature of homosexuality and the feelings of one who is involved in a relationship that can never be mutually satisfying. Although this was the situation with Heidi and Jeffrey in *Just Be Gorgeous*, the deception in TJ and Noli's case makes their relationship more intense and takes the reader deeper into the complexity of both characters' psyches.

Rather than recount a story that has already happened, as Wersba often does, this time she starts at what turns out to be the end of the story and the beginning of the protagonist's changed life. In chapter one Noli sees TJ, who has caused her so much anger and heartache, walking down a street in Sag Harbor. The next 19 chapters provide exposition detailing why Noli now wants to avoid TJ. Chapter 20 returns to the beginning of the story, the point at which TJ turns and confronts her. Noli responds by making a clean break with an old love that could cripple her for life. In the final chapter, she begins to come into her own. This technique of starting at the end adds to the book's intensity because until the final chapter one is uncertain how the situation will be resolved. The reader does not know that the protagonist is going to be all right as the reader does in the case of Albert Scully, who introduces himself as someone who "used to be quite a mess." Instead, we wait to see if Noli will indeed find her way home.

Wersba's inspiration for *Whistle Me Home* came when a new voice entered her consciousness. Although reminiscent of the voice of Albert Scully, which inspired *The Dream Watcher*, this was not the voice of a teenager. It was, rather, the voice of an intimate narrator. Using this voice posed a welcome challenge to Wersba, who felt she needed a different approach in her writing. As Wersba puts it, "This voice was a new music, and that made the book come to life."[2]

Reviewers were quick to comment on the voice in *Whistle Me Home*. Roger Sutton, of *Horn Book,* commended Wersba for "abjuring the current preference for the first-person or some other gesture toward 'teen-talk,' " and using a "dispassionate omniscient narration that both underplays and underlines the story."[3] In a starred review in *Booklist,* Ilene Cooper said Wersba's use of the present tense was "inspired, giving an immediacy to events that, though in the past, are still crashing around in Noli's brain."[4] Sutton noted that "the dialogue, while sometimes passionate, is that of two well-spoken young adults. It's the swanky, I'm-a-grown-up kind of prose that we maybe took for granted in the old days of the new realism" (Sutton, 331).

The American Library Association's (ALA's) Young Adult Library Services Association (YALSA) selected *Whistle Me Home* for both its 1998 Best Books for Young Adults[5] and its Books for Reluctant Readers (known as the Quick Picks for Young Adult Readers)[6] lists. *Whistle Me Home* was also selected as an honor book by the Society of School Librarians International (SSLI) in the category of Secondary Language Arts, 7–12 Novels for 1997.[7]

Critical acclaim for both the literary style and content of Wersba's newest novel indicates that she remains an effective writer for young adults, handling problem novels topics in an engaging manner without being didactic. In other words, she still has it after all these years.

8. Here We Go Again!: Familiar Faces, Situations, Places, and Themes

A psychologist friend of Wersba's once pointed out that she keeps telling the same story over and over. Although this observation initially surprised Wersba, it is true. In her 16 young adult novels, she is essentially retelling the story of a socially isolated teenager who is mentored by a person outside his or her immediate family and is therefore encouraged to pursue dreams and develop a unique potential. This is, of course, Wersba's own story, but it's one that touches a universal desire to replace despair with hope. Although this story forms the heart of each novel, the circumstances and settings in which it manifests itself vary in such a way that it does indeed seem like a new story each time Wersba tells it. At the same time, familiar characters, situations, places, and themes recur throughout the various novels, providing "Wersba touches" that many readers have come to welcome and anticipate.

Characters

In addition to Wersba's recurring basic story, a fascinating aspect of her work is the way in which characters with similar personalities, problems, and interests enter and reenter her novels. All of her protagonists, from Albert Scully to Noli Brown, are misfits, loners who differ from their peers so markedly that they are generally ostracized. Sometimes the difference is due, at least partially, to a physical characteristic such as Harvey Beaumont's and

Tyler Woodruff's lack of height, Rita Formica's excess weight, or Heidi Rosenbloom's, J. F. McAllister's, and Noli Brown's boyish appearance. Sometimes it's an artistic or aesthetic pursuit such as Albert Scully's interest in gardening, David Marks's desire to be a painter, and Tyler Woodruff's passion for photography that sets them apart. Sometimes it's a quality difficult to define, but one that results in a lack of self-esteem, as in the cases of Archie Smith and Justin Weinberg. Wersba's protagonists frequently possess some combination of these traits along with a self-deprecating attitude. They perceive themselves as different from other teens, and although they do not wish to be conventional, they suffer in their isolation.

Wersba's characters do not remain completely isolated, and herein often lies the novel's plot. Someone, in most cases an older person, steps into a depressed teenager's life, throws him or her a reassuring lifeline that changes the teen's life for the better, and then leaves. Although Wersba's protagonists have much in common, the people they encounter differ greatly, offering a wonderful array of fascinating characters. *The Dream Watcher*'s Mrs. Woodfin was the first of the influential older characters, followed by such notables as Hadley Norman, Chandler Brown, Harold Murth, Jeffrey Collins, Lionel Moss, and Kerry Brown.

Some of these human lifelines are nearer the protagonist's own age: Maggie Carroll, for instance, is one year older than David Marks, just as Mitzi Gerrard is one grade ahead of Tyler Woodruff; Polo Quinn is the same age as Archie Smith, and TJ Baker and Noli Brown are both high-school juniors. However, these characters of similar age who act as a lifeline are always more worldly and usually more emotionally mature than the protagonists. Although most of these "helpful others" physically disappear from the protagonists' lives, Arnold Bromberg remains with Rita Formica. Heidi Rosenbloom and Harvey Beaumont also stay together, but they have each had previous experiences with older people that have helped them in early adolescence. In each case, however, the protagonist emerges with an elevated self-concept, and no matter how painful that process may have been, he or she usually has an improved outlook on life.

Although they are loners, not all of Wersba's characters are necessarily friendless before encountering their life-changing person. For example, Rick Heaton discusses art continually with David Marks, and Marylou Brown assists J. F. McAllister in her scheme to raise money for Harold Murth. Likewise, Bruno Kaufmann encourages Justin Weinberg to pursue Kerry Brown, and Nicole Sicard helps Rita Formica, up to a point, in her plan to attract Robert Swann. Several protagonists have had a good friend move away, a situation that often exacerbates their loneliness: Archie Smith's one and only friend, Clifford Tromblay, moved to Hawaii three years before the story begins. Rita Formica's friend, Corry Brown, recently moved to New York, and Heidi Rosenbloom's friend, Veronica Bangs, lives in California.

In addition to being loners, Wersba's protagonists are often close to the arts. Most have some type of aesthetic appreciation and many have artistic aspirations. It is not unusual for Wersba's New York City characters to meet in the Metropolitan Museum of Art or for any of her characters to discuss literature. Albert Scully loves literature; David Marks devotes himself to painting; Steven Harper longs to be a poet; J. F. McAllister teaches herself to play the harmonica; Harvey Beaumont writes short stories and later pursues a career in photography; Tyler Woodruff devotes himself to wildlife photography; Rita Formica wants to be a writer; Heidi Rosenbloom develops an appreciation for quality literature; Archie Smith is an avid reader; Justin Weinberg wants to become an actor; and Noli Brown is an old-film buff. Secondary characters also aspire to artistic endeavors. Mrs. Woodfin was an actress in her fantasy life; Chandler Brown hopes to become an actress; Jeffrey Collins strives to be a Broadway star; Arnold Bromberg plays the organ; Joel Greenberg's brother is the author of a bestselling novel; Bruno Kaufmann hopes to be writer; and TJ Baker has acted in an off-Broadway play.

As well as being artistic and surrounded by the artistically inclined, Wersba's protagonists are intelligent, sometimes even intellectual, though they may not do well in school. All of them, except for Albert Scully, Steven Harper, Archie Smith, and Noli Brown, attend private prep schools. The boys attend Spencer

School or Lawrence School for Boys if they live in New York City, or Southampton Country-Day if they live in the Hamptons; the girls attend Spencer or Miss Howlett's. But no matter what school they attend, their schoolwork usually suffers because they are apathetic to the school milieu and spend their time pursuing artistic interests. Albert Scully, David Marks, Harvey Beaumont, Rita Formica, and Justin Weinberg all fall into this category of underachievers. Archie Smith is too depressed and lonely to apply himself; Heidi Rosenbloom would rather spend time with dogs than her books; and Noli Brown's drinking usurps any interest in school. Tyler Woodruff maintains an A average, but Joel Greenberg is one of the few conventionally good students in Wersba's books.

Joel is also unusual because he is trying to attract his parents' attention by being a model son. All the other main characters, except Steven Harper and Noli Brown, suffer their parents' disappointment, even wrath, because they do not want to go to college and become successful by their parents' definitions. Steven Harper is already studying literature at a local community college, a pursuit his father considers frivolous. Noli Brown's father does not think it important for a girl to attend college, but her mother would support Noli in this endeavor if Noli herself were at all interested.

The adults in Wersba's books demonstrate a mixture of neglectful and overbearing parenting behaviors. J. F.'s father, for example, is so busy with his business ventures he rarely sees her, and J. F.'s mother, except for being openly disgusted by her daughter's androgynous appearance, is too preoccupied with her own appearance to be an effective parent. Roger Smith is also preoccupied, but in a more benign way, with his study of P. L. Travers. On the domineering side, self-made successes Leo Marks and Leonard Rosenbloom insist David and Heidi attend prestigious colleges that will provide the education and status they themselves lack. Wanting her daughter to marry well, Shirley Rosenbloom is obsessed with Heidi's hair and clothing, and tries to make her look feminine. Mrs. Brown and Noli also battle over Noli's refusal to appear feminine. Mrs. Scully pushes her Albert toward conventional success by warning him against becoming an alcoholic like his father. Upper-class George Woodruff, George Weinberg, and Muriel Beaumont all manage to be both neglectful and tyrannical parents. All three are self-absorbed at the expense of their children but nonetheless expect them to follow family tradition by attending prestigious colleges and going into business or medicine.

Many times the husband or wife of a neglectful or domineering parent will play the peacemaker. Dolly Marks does this when she begs David to make amends with his father before he dies; Katherine Woodruff attempts to intervene for Tyler regarding his interest in wild birds; Mr. Beaumont suggests Harvey try to understand how unloved his mother feels; Mrs. Formica visits Rita when Tony Formica refuses to see her; Harold Brown tries to ameliorate the hard feelings between Noli and her mother by talking about the baby she lost. Harvey Beaumont's father, however, is the only parent who succeeds in the peacemaking endeavor. When a spouse does not play the role of arbitrator, sometimes another adult, perhaps an aunt or uncle, will take on these peacemaking efforts. Aunt Theo does this for Justin in *Life Is What Happens*.

With all the problems Wersba's characters experience, it is not surprising that her novels are fraught with mental-health experts. Sometimes these professionals are completely ineffective, as in the case of Albert Scully's overly familiar school psychologist, J. F. McAllister's eclectic psychiatrist, Dr. Waingloss, and Rita Formica's unsympathetic weight therapist, Dr. Strawberry. In other cases, the therapist is helpful, but that help is never openly acknowledged. For example, even though Archie Smith will never show his notebook to Dr. Gutman, composing the entries, as his psychiatrist suggested, has a therapeutic effect on Archie. Similarly, the school psychologist who insists Noli Brown go to AA meetings helps her even though Noli never formally acknowledges this assistance. Rita Formica is rather unusual because she appreciates Ms. Perlman, the social worker who helps the Formicas and Arnold Bromberg work out the complexities of their relationships.

Just as it is not uncommon for a Wersba character to see a therapist, it is not unusual for a Wersba character to be an alcoholic.

Both Mr. Scully and Mrs. Woodfin's drinking problems are mentioned in *Dream Watcher,* and Tony Formica starts to drink heavily during the course of Rita's developing relationship with Arnold Bromberg. Chandler Brown's alcoholism is described more fully in *Carnival,* and she says she intends to get help from AA when she returns to Michigan. In *Crazy Vanilla,* Katherine Woodruff's dependence on alcohol is obvious; toward the end of that novel, her son Tyler helps her realize her problem and mentions that he attends AA meetings with her. These are all secondary characters; however, teenage alcoholic Noli Brown is the protagonist in *Whistle,* making the topic of alcoholism a central concern in Wersba's most recent novel.

Alcoholics may frequently appear, but writers abound even more in Wersba's novels. Some—Steven Harper, Harvey Beaumont, Rita Formica, Arnold Bromberg, and Bruno Kaufmann—are literary hopefuls. Others—Hadley Norman, Samuel and Bradley Brown, Doris Morris (alias Amanda Starcross), Jerry Malone (alias Victor Colorado), Nora Thurston Quadrangle, Christopher Quinn, and JJ Greenberg—have already achieved literary success of varying sorts. Wersba uses this wide array of writers to comment on various literary genres as well as to address the importance of writing, both as a profession and as a personally gratifying pursuit. In addition, some of her best-drawn secondary characters are the writers whose works she parodies. Their presence adds an enticing dimension to Wersba's own writing.

Time Periods

Most of Wersba's protagonists are in the same general situation: they are lonely teenagers at odds with one or more parent. However, the particulars of their circumstances vary according to the characters they come in contact with, the time period the story takes place in, and the economic status of the character's family.

Albert Scully finds himself in the middle of an early 1960s suburban dream turned nightmare. His mother expects his father to be the dutiful breadwinner and provide her with a beautiful home equipped with all the modern conveniences extolled in *House Beautiful*. As the family struggles financially to hold fast to this dream, Albert struggles emotionally to develop independence from a domineering mother. The Beatles, Lady Bird Johnson, and pop art are all part of the stage on which the story of *The Dream Watcher* takes place. In *Run Softly, Go Fast,* bell-bottomed, sandal-footed, longhaired David Marks engages in a battle with his wealthy father as he tries to gain control over his own life. Drugs, the Vietnam War, conscientious objectors, and the hippie lifestyle figure prominently in Wersba's second novel, which is steeped in the counterculture of the late '60s. *The Country of the Heart* is loosely tied to this same time period by Steven Harper's reference to his younger sister, who has adopted the life of a vagabond hippie. However, the intensity with which Steven writes of the love affair that saved him from the smallmindedness of his anti-intellectual father strongly reflects the spirit of the times. Both *Country* and *Run Softly* may seem overwritten by today's standards, but their styles masterfully capture the ambience of the turbulent, introspective '60s.

References to Gay Lib, transactional analysis, and existentialism place *Tunes for a Small Harmonica* in the mid- to late 1960s. However, J. F. McAllister's situation is most strongly influenced by her affluent family's emphasis on convention. She is determined to remain outside the mold they have set for her. Harvey Beaumont the Third, of *The Carnival in My Mind,* also comes from a moneyed background, and his eccentric mother's passion for Irish setters strongly shapes the circumstances of his life. Prostitution and alcoholism are introduced in *Carnival*, although these social concerns do not have a particular relationship to the novel's time period, which seems to be the early to mid-1970s. AIDS, on the other hand, is a social issue with a definite beginning; by mentioning it in *Crazy Vanilla*, Wersba situates that novel in the early '80s.

Although the Sag Harbor trilogy is set in the '80s, the main effect the time period has on Rita Formica's situation seems to be the ease with which she suggests that she and Arnold live together before they marry. Her parents are appalled, once again, that Rita has chosen a life outside their middle-class values. Heidi Rosenbloom's and Harvey Beaumont's mothers, who both come from privileged backgrounds, have the same reaction when their children move in together. But Heidi and Harvey, like Rita, have grown up with an acceptance of this premarital step. The Heidi books also evoke an '80s tenor through their inclusion of openly gay characters and an exploration of the life of the homeless in New York City.

The Best Place to Live Is the Ceiling is a bit more difficult to date since much of it takes place in Switzerland, but the punk appearance of the teens in Zürich places it in the early 1980s. However, it is not the time period, but rather his father's poor financial status as a teacher and solitary life as an intellectual that shapes the circumstances leading to Archie Smith's adventure. *You'll Never Guess the End*, however, is clearly a '90s book with its postmodern literary allusions and its characters suggestive of recognizable New York types—all of which make Joel Greenberg's life quite exciting. Video-rental stores, postmodern steel and glass architecture, and the mention of sex-changes establish an early-1990s setting for *Life Is What Happens*, and it's a film video that makes affluent Justin Weinberg aware of Kerry Brown, the star who changes his life. Teenage alcoholism certainly is not new in the '90s, but the backward-worn baseball caps that Noli, TJ, and Walker wear; Noli's brazen, profanity-laden speech patterns; and the R.E.M. concert they attend show them to be teens of this period. TJ's need to hide his homosexuality causes Noli much anguish, but the harsh reality is that even in the 1990s most adolescents have little tolerance for homosexual peers.

As each of Wersba's protagonists manages to find someone who can help him or her grow toward maturity and independence, Wersba takes readers on a sociological tour across three decades. Because she adapts her story for teens in each decade, her underlying story could be called a tale for several generations, not just because it spans a 30-year period, but because her readership has consisted of teens, young adults in their 20s, adults old enough to be the parents of teenagers, and adults old enough to have teenage grandchildren. Some of these readers identify with

Wersba's teens, some with their parents, and some with both as the universal tension between adolescents and their parents plays out in the circumstances found in Wersba's novels.

Places

Not only do situations recur in Wersba's novels, but so do places. J. F. McAllister, Harvey Beaumont, Heidi Rosenbloom, and Joel Greenberg all live in New York City. Readers become familiar with the geography of New York City by accompanying these characters as they walk dogs in Central Park, visit the Museum of Modern Art, attend performances in Greenwich Village, have tea or champagne at the Plaza Hotel, shop in exclusive Fifth Avenue stores, busk in the Broadway theater district, search the city for apartments or missing persons, and take numerous cab rides, often with a dog or two for company. Because the city is accessible to Wersba's highly allowanced characters—many of whom live near or frequent the same places—and because Wersba describes her settings with careful attention to detail, it is possible for one to become fairly well acquainted with, even fond of, New York City just from reading her nine New York novels.

Wersba's works can create a similar familiarity with Sag Harbor and the Hamptons. When Tyler Woodruff, Rita Formica, Justin Weinberg, and Noli Brown begin their stories by saying they live in Sag Harbor, or one of the other Hamptons, and proceed to describe the physical location and social atmosphere of these towns, anyone who has read even one other Wersba novel set on the east end of Long Island begins to feel at home. Whether one is encountering them for the first or the sixth time, the shoreline, the ponds, the wild birds, the piers, the beaches, the small businesses, and the villages themselves always form appealing backdrops for Wersba's Hampton novels. Wersba's artful depiction of the beauty and serenity of the area makes it easy to understand why the families of so many of her New York City characters have a second home in the Hamptons.

In Wersba's earlier novels the movement was generally from the city to the Hamptons, as when Tyler Woodruff's father came to spend weekends with his family in their North Haven home. However, in her latest novels Hampton dwellers take advantage of the educational and entertainment opportunities offered in New York: Justin Weinberg wants to attend acting school in New York and live in Water Mill on the weekends, and Noli and TJ celebrate New Year's Day with a trip to New York City.

One other location that figures in Wersba's novels frequently enough to provide reader familiarity is Zürich, Switzerland. First the "Zürichoise" Arnold Bromberg of *Love Is the Crooked Thing* guides Rita around this city that has become his home. Then, four novels later in *Ceiling*, Melina Mendelsohn gives Archie Smith a formal introduction to the city. Polo Quinn later shows him Zürich from the perspective of a teenage street person. Couple these tours with Rita's and Archie's own perceptive observations and Wersba supplies readers abundant information about this fascinating European city. Indeed, the Fraumünster, St. Peter's Square, the Water Chapel, the River Limmat, the Limmatquai, and the Neiderdorf have all become familiar places by Wersba's second Zürich novel. In addition, Archie's adventure takes him into the Alps, making Davos part of the Wersbian tour of Switzerland.

Interestingly, Wersba mentions Zürich and Davos before any of her characters actually go there. For instance, in *Fat,* Nicole Sicard tells Robert Swann that Rita skis in Davos yearly and was once involved in a spy ring in Zürich. Readers accustomed to the way ideas and places weave in and out of Wersba's books might well expect one of her characters to travel to New Zealand. After all, various Wersba characters from Albert Scully on have dreamed of visiting that country. When Justin Weinberg plans to fly to New Zealand, it would be in keeping with Wersba's plot patterns to have him actually board the plane. And had Wersba been to New Zealand herself, he most likely would have carried out his plans. But Wersba only writes about places she knows well, so Justin did not go to Wanganui, New Zealand; instead, Kerry Brown came to the Hamptons.

Themes

Just as the places Wersba has known and loved form the backdrop for her novels, Wersba's beliefs create thematic undercurrents that run through her works. The first of these is the importance of being oneself. Mrs. Woodfin imparts this idea to Albert Scully when she discusses the acceptability, even advisability, of being different, of marching to a different drummer. This is the basic message Wersba's mentors convey to the lonely misfits they seek to encourage. Of course being oneself implies self-knowledge and self-acceptance, so these are also central concepts in the novels. Jeffrey Collins uses himself as a model for encouraging Heidi Rosenbloom to be herself. Jeffrey is gay and does not try to hide it. He calls her crew cut "adorable" and admires the secondhand, man's overcoat she wears. With these comments, Jeffrey brings up two aspects of being oneself, one's sexuality and one's appearance.

The question of sexual orientation arises in most of Wersba's novels, beginning in *Run Softly* when Leo Marks calls Rick Heaton a queer and throws him out of the house and ending, so far at least, with *Whistle* when Noli Brown breaks up with TJ Baker and calls him a fag. Through characters such as Tyler Woodruff's elder brother, Cameron, Jeffrey Collins, and TJ Baker, it becomes clear that homosexuality is not a choice; it is simply part of who one is. Jeffrey and Cameron cannot and do not want to change who they are. Difficult as society may make it for them, each embraces his homosexuality as part of his identity. TJ is probably much like Cameron was in high school, popular and still in the closet. Self-knowledge is present, but self-acceptance has yet to develop fully. As an adult, Cameron is confident in being himself, thereby providing a positive example of a young man who is successfully unconventional.

Expressing one's individuality through one's appearance, a second aspect of being oneself, is another question that arises in most of Wersba's novels. Leo Marks's last words to David are "Get a haircut"; Shirley Rosenbloom continually buys Heidi makeup and frilly blouses that Heidi will never wear. Because appearance is conventionally associated with gender, the way teens, particularly girls, dress in Wersba's novels is often a source of conflict between the parents and their children. Most of Wersba's adolescent girls dress and wear their hair like boys. J. F. and Heidi do not do this because it is fashionable; they just prefer an androgynous look. Of course Heidi did cut her hair as an act of rebellion against her mother, just as Noli burned her dresses. Noli's haircut, on the other hand, is a result of her extreme unhappiness, perhaps even a form of self-mutilation. Appearance is a complex issue for adolescents, but at some point dressing conventionally or unconventionally becomes each individual's choice, a statement about who one is.

A theme closely related to being oneself involves the importance of following a personal dream, even when parents disapprove. Wersba's characters come to understand this concept at varying points in the novels, but it is always mentioned in one way or another. At the conclusion of *Dream Watcher* Albert Scully finally understands the special gift Mrs. Woodfin has given him by suggesting he forgo college, even if his mother objects, and pursue his dream, whether it be operating a tugboat or moving to New Zealand. Tyler Woodruff, Heidi Rosenbloom (in *Just Be Gorgeous*), and Harvey Beaumont (in *Carnival*) also begin to visualize their dreams for the future at the end of their novels. Other characters, such as David Marks and Steven Harper, pursue their artistic dreams throughout the course of their stories, much to their parents' dismay. In an extreme instance, Archie Smith's dream of foreign adventure is actually fulfilled within the course of the novel itself.

Sometimes the importance of dreams is demonstrated through parents who have suffered from a dream unfulfilled. Leo Marks and Mr. Scully both wanted to be airline pilots; Tony Formica wanted to be a race-car driver; Mrs. Brown wanted to be an interior designer; George Weinberg wanted to build yachts; Kathy Woodruff wanted to be an actress; and George Woodruff wanted to be a doctor. They all gave up their dreams because their parents or circumstances demanded they do so, and they all regret this decision. The irony is that most of them insist their own children relinquish their dreams as well. In a few cases this makes the parents more sympathetic, but in many it only hardens them against their children's aspirations. Because he knows both his parents gave up their dreams, Tyler Woodruff is fully aware that most people do not get what they want out of life. Realizing that dreams are important, he knows he must be determined if he is to pursue his heart's desire and become a professional wildlife photographer.   *

The use of deception is frequently involved as protagonists begin to understand or pursue their dreams. Although lying and sneaking are often regarded as character defects, many of Wersba's protagonists routinely forge notes on a parent's stationery, provide false information about their whereabouts, search people's personal records or belongings, or invent elaborate stories about themselves. These deceptive behaviors are not condoned, but simply accepted as common teenage conduct. On the other hand, other deceptions in which the adults or teens engage—Mrs. Woodfin's fabricated acting career, Leo Marks's infidelity, Chandler Brown's prostitution, Marilyn Schumacher's bogus kidnapping, Polo Quinn's feigned promiscuous past, TJ Baker's heterosexual facade—are more troublesome. These behaviors cause the protagonists to question the importance of truth and their relationships with the people who deceive them. Whether the truth is always necessary or lying is always harmful is a thematic question that Wersba frequently revisits.

The importance of animals in the lives of humans is another major theme running throughout Wersba's work. Unhappy relationships with parents and peers often cause Wersba's characters to find comfort in the animal world. Albert Scully's cat is a source of solace to him; Heidi Rosenbloom believes only her dog Happy truly loves her; Tyler Woodruff grows overly attached to the wild birds he photographs; Joel Greenberg is quite fond of Sherlock; and Alice seems to be Noli Brown's only companion. However, Hadley Norman and Muriel Beaumont, two eccentric adults, probably do love animals more than they love people. Even characters who don't devote some aspect of their lives to animals hold them in high esteem. Lionel Moss, for instance, buys presents for Happy and MacGregor; Jeffrey Collins gives Happy his hamburger. Archie Smith knows exactly how to treat each of his father's 12 cats. Sometimes animals serve as a conduit for expressing a character's feelings: Mr. Smith tells Archie the cats missed him when he was in Switzerland; Holmes informs Harvey Beaumont the dogs will miss him if he moves out of the apartment. Heidi Rosenbloom does this too when she notifies Harvey that the dogs missed him when he did not visit her in her barbershop abode. Thus animals not only help Wersba's characters cope with their own loneliness, they also assist them in their relationships with other humans.

That there is always hope is a foremost theme with Wersba. Her novels never begin on a happy note, as her characters are generally immersed in adolescent angst, often to the point of feeling suicidal. But by the end of each novel, life has improved, showing that emotional turmoil is a normal part of human development, self-esteem is achievable, and, in some cases, parent/ child relationships can be mutually satisfying. Often these realizations come in the form of epiphanies at the end of the novel when the protagonist reflects upon what has taken place in his or her life. Some of Wersba's characters, like Rita Formica and Heidi Rosenbloom, are graced with a wry sense of humor to help them through the rough times; others, such as Steven Harper and David Marks, have an artist's perspective to help them make sense of their world. And because the natural world enables many to transcend hopelessness, the swans, geese, and egrets that fly through Wersba's books symbolize the resilience of the human spirit and ever-present hope.

Hallmarks of the Wersba Style

With so many recurring characteristics, one might wonder why Wersba's writing has not grown tiresome to her readers. But in fact, just the opposite is true. Wersba may be relating the same story again and again, but as with any story, it's all in the telling. And Wersba is such a gifted storyteller that readers often feel they are encountering old friends seen in a new light, as her lovable misfits, lonely oddballs, witty narrators, and quirky characters reappear in her stories. In fact, some of the behaviors and phrases might even be termed *Wersbaisms*.

These include, for example, angry fathers throwing the Christmas tree out the window; mothers valuing virginity as though it were the Hope Diamond; characters with a weakness for taxis; teens tipping the taxi driver too much; admirers calling an unusual person *un original*; girls thinking they look like female impersonators; children declining trips to Europe with their parents; lovers seeing themselves as two sides of a single coin; and characters having Brown for their last name. Names, words, and works of famous people dance through so many of the books that Woody Allen, Henry David Thoreau, George Sand, Chopin, Stevie Smith, George Bernard Shaw, Tennessee Williams, Arthur Miller, and Greta Garbo are warmly greeted with immediate recognition. Again, this familiarity is part of the enjoyment of reading a Wersba novel.

Conclusion

Because Wersba's novels have so much to offer, it is puzzling that she has not received the recognition she deserves as one of the first and enduring writers in the genre.[1] The quality of her writing is evident, but as several reviewers have noted, Wersba's books are not for everyone, and that's not bad. Readers who appreciate Wersba are often intelligent, artistic, and individualistic, like her characters and like Wersba herself. Although enjoyable, humorous, thought-provoking, and reassuring, Wersba's plots and characters do not, perhaps, have the mass appeal that makes books popular with many teens. This, of course, is true of many authors, but several other factors need to be considered.

One is the controversial subject matter of her books. Although her books are literary, many of the topics she addresses, sexuality in particular, make the books more suitable for private reading than for whole class study, so teachers are not apt to use them in the classroom. In addition, many of her novels are generally recommended for older teens, and as experts in the field are well aware, this age group is becoming an endangered species in terms of young adult literature. Marketing is generally geared to middle-school-aged teens because their teachers are more accepting of the genre and middle schoolers are not as pressured to read the classics as are their high-school counterparts.

But even when teachers elect to study a particular topic such as AIDS or homelessness through young adult literature, they may inadvertently overlook Wersba's books because they are not simply topical problem novels. Many teachers and librarians are unaware that Wersba addresses contemporary issues naturally within the context of a complex, realistic story involving teenage problems and relationships. Thus, for example, when a list of books with gay characters appears, *Crazy Vanilla* or *Just Be Gorgeous* will probably not be on it. And again, this is not bad. It just means that Wersba's books are hard to pigeonhole.

Although Wersba does want to reach people through her books, she writes first for herself, trying to work through, reshape, and learn from her own childhood and adolescence. Using recognizable time periods may make the books seem dated, but she prefers to retell her story as it might occur in a particular setting. Her artistic integrity will not allow her to make choices or changes merely because they would increase her sales; she is not interested in selling books at all costs, and does not pander to marketing strategies.

In her earlier years, Wersba spoke and signed books at schools and professional conferences. But because she is shy and public speaking makes her nervous, she now rarely makes public appearances. However, because of the rapid increase in the number of authors who write young adult literature, those who appear at conferences, make school visits, and have speeches published in professional journals often gain the attention of teachers and librarians. Although understandable, Wersba's absence from this professional scene is, perhaps, another reason she has not been as widely recognized as one might expect.

She does, however, appear in all the major reference works, old and new, on children's and young adult authors.[2] Scholars have long recognized her contribution to the field of young adult literature as significant. But more important to Wersba than widespread recognition or numerous awards are the individual readers to whom her writing speaks personally, passionately, and brings comfort. Like her characters, Wersba is a person who is determined to follow *her* dream, be it acting, writing, or operating a small press. She seeks first to please herself, and, of course—as we have learned from reading her books—this is not bad at all.

Notes and References

1. Barbara Wersba: Loner, Actress, Writer, Teacher, Publisher, Friend

1. Paul Janeczko, "Barbara Wersba," in *From Writers to Students: The Pleasures and Pains of Writing,* ed. M. Jerry Weiss (Newark, Del.: International Reading Association, 1970), 96; hereafter cited in text.

2. This chapter's otherwise uncredited quotations and paraphrases from Wersba are from an interview conducted by the author at Wersba's North Haven home on 30 May 1993 or from telephone interviews conducted with Wersba on 19 February 1995, 19 June 1995, 20 August 1996, and 4 October 1996.

3. Charlotte Zolotow, personal interview by author, at the Dorset Hotel, New York City, 27 May 1993.

4. Adele Sarkissian, ed., *Something about the Author Autobiography Series* (Detroit: Gale Research, 1986), 2:293; hereafter cited in text.

5. Commire, Anne, ed., *Something about the Author: Facts and Pictures about Authors and Illustrators of Books for Young People* (Detroit: Gale Research, 1990), 58:180; hereafter cited in text.

6. Refna Wilkins, telephone interview by author, 12 July 1995. Wilkins is currently an editor at Putnam's.

7. Barbara Wersba, "On Discovering Janet Frame," in *The Inward Sun: Celebrating the Life and Work of Janet Frame,* ed. Elizabeth Alley (Thorndon, New Zealand: Daphne Brasell, 1994), 165; Alley selected and

edited the contributions to this book for Frame's 70th birthday.

8. Barbara Wersba, "Barbara Wersba—as a Writer," *Top of the News*, June 1975, 428.

9. Publisher's brochure, Atheneum, 1970.

10. Julie Fallowfield, telephone interview by author, 13 November 1996.

2. *Finding Oneself:* The Dream Watcher;
Run Softly, Go Fast; *and* The Country of the Heart

1. Barbara Wersba, *The Dream Watcher* (New York: Atheneum, 1968), 1; hereafter cited in text by page number.

2. This chapter's otherwise uncredited quotations and paraphrases from Wersba are from telephone interviews conducted by the author with Wersba on 19 June 1995 and 20 August 1995.

3. Paul Zindel, *The Pigman* (New York: Harper & Row, 1968); S. E. Hinton, *The Outsiders* (New York: Delacorte, 1967); Robert Lipsyte, *The Contender* (New York: Harper & Row, 1967); Ann Head, *Mr. and Mrs. BoJo Jones* (New York: Putnam's, 1967).

4. Zena Sutherland, review of *The Dream Watcher*, *Saturday Review of Literature*, 9 November 1968, 69; hereafter cited in text.

5. Pamela Bragg, review of *The Dream Watcher*, *Publishers Weekly*, 18 November 1968, 86.

6. Virginia Haviland, review of *The Dream Watcher*, *Horn Book*, October 1968, 567.

7. John Weston, review of *The Dream Watcher*, *New York Times Book Review*, part 2, 3 November 1968, 2.

8. Polly Goodwin, review of *The Dream Watcher*, *The Washington Post*, 3 November 1969, Book World section, 18.

9. Diane Gersoni Stavn, "The Skirts in Fiction about Boys: In a Maxi Mess," *School Library Journal*, January 1971, 283.

10. Maggie Parish, "The Mother as Witch, Fairy God-mother, Survivor, or Victim in Contemporary Realistic Fiction for Young Adults," *English Journal*, October 1979, 103.
11. Jerry J. Watson, "A Positive Image of the Elderly in Literature for Children," *The Reading Teacher*, April 1981, 795.
12. Unsigned review of *The Dream Watcher*, *Time* magazine, 13 December 1968, 2.
13. Laura Polla Scanlon, review of *The Dream Watcher*, *Commonweal*, 22 November 1968, 289.
14. Barbara Wersba, *Run Softly, Go Fast* (New York: Atheneum, 1970), 153; hereafter cited in text by page number.
15. Sheryl B. Andrews, "Book: For Children at Christmas: Ages Eight to Twelve," review of *Run Softly, Go Fast*, *Horn Book*, December 1970, 624.
16. Nancy Garden, review of *Run Softly, Go Fast*, *American Observer*, 4 October 1971. Page number unknown.
17. John Rowe Townsend, review of *Run Softly, Go Fast*, *New York Times Book Review*, 22 November 1970, 38.
18. Roger Sutton, "The Critical Myth: Realistic YA Novels," *School Library Journal*, November 1982, 34.
19. "Outstanding Books of the Year," *New York Times*, 8 November 1970, 34.
20. American Library Association, "Best Books for Young Adults, 1970," *Booklist*, 1 April 1971, 655.
21. Alleen Pace Nilsen and Kenneth L. Donelson, "Young Adults and Their Reading," *Literature for Today's Young Adults*, 4th ed. (New York: HarperCollins College, 1993), 17.
22. Ken Donelson, "Fifty YA Books Out of the Past Still Worth Reading; or, Enjoyment Is There *If* You Search for It," *ALAN Review* (a publication of the Assembly on Literature for Adolescents of the National Council of Teachers of English), Fall 1986, 63.

23. American Library Association, "Top One Hundred Countdown: Best of the Best Books for Young Adults," *Booklist*, 15 October 1994, 413.

24. Elizabeth Poe, "What about Those Out of Print Books?" *ALAN Review*, Fall 1993, 57.

25. Angela Leone, "Booksearch: Out-of-Print Books That Should Still Be in Print," *English Journal*, December 1991, 90–91.

26. Barbara Wersba, *The Country of the Heart* (New York: Atheneum, 1975), 10–11; hereafter cited in text by page number.

27. Mary Silva Cosgrave, review of *The Country of the Heart, Horn Book,* December 1975, 618.

28. Georgess McHargue, review of *The Country of the Heart*, *New York Times Book Review*, 4 January 1976, 8.

**3. *Accepting Oneself:* Tunes for a Small Harmonica,
The Carnival in My Mind, *and* Crazy Vanilla**

1. Barbara Wersba, *Tunes for a Small Harmonica* (New York: Harper & Row, 1976), 57; hereafter cited in text by page number.

2. This chapter's otherwise uncredited quotations and paraphrases from Wersba are from telephone interviews conducted by the author on 3 July 1995 and 19 February 1996.

3. G. Robert Carlsen, Connie Bennett, and Anne Harker, "1977 Books for Young Adults Book Poll," *English Journal*, January 1978, 92.

4. Unsigned review of *Tunes for a Small Harmonica*, *Booklist*, 15 September 1976, 139.

5. Zena Sutherland, review of *Tunes for a Small Harmonica, Bulletin of the Center for Children's Books*, February 1977, 99.

6. Barbara Wersba, *The Carnival in My Mind* (New York: Harper & Row, 1982), 4; hereafter cited in text by page number.

7. Paul Heins, review of *The Carnival in My Mind, Horn Book*, December 1982, 662–63.

8. Unsigned review of *The Carnival in My Mind*, *Bulletin of the Center for Children's Books*, October 1982, 39.

9. Barbara Wersba, *Crazy Vanilla* (New York: Harper & Row, 1986), 1; hereafter cited in text by page number.

10. Marijo Duncan, review of *Crazy Vanilla*, *Voice of Youth Advocates (VOYA)*, August/October 1986, 137.

11. Unsigned review of *Crazy Vanilla*, *Kirkus*, 1 November 1986, 1653.

12. Zena Sutherland, review of *Crazy Vanilla*, *Bulletin of the Center for Children's Books*, March 1987, 137.

4. Unconventional Romances: The Saga of Rita Formica

1. Barbara Wersba, *Fat: A Love Story* (New York: Harper & Row, 1987), 57; hereafter cited in text by page number.

2. Barbara Wersba, *Love Is the Crooked Thing* (New York: Harper & Row, 1987), 104; hereafter cited in text by page number.

3. Barbara Wersba, *Beautiful Losers* (New York: Harper & Row, 1988), 32; hereafter cited in text by page number.

4. This chapter's otherwise uncredited quotations and paraphrases from Wersba are from a telephone interview conducted by the author on 19 February 1996.

5. Thomas Clavin, "Tyler in Sag Harbor," *Southampton Press*, 25 December 1986, B5.

6. Diane Roback, review of *Fat: A Love Story*, *Publishers Weekly,* 12 June 1987, 86.

7. Hazel Rochman, review of *Fat: A Love Story*, *Booklist*, 1 June 1987, 1517.

8. Hazel Rochman, review of *Love Is the Crooked Thing*, *Booklist*, 1 October 1987, 255.

9. Diane Roback, review of *Love Is the Crooked Thing*, *Publishers Weekly,* 9 October 1987, 89–90.

10. Hazel Rochman, review of *Beautiful Losers*, *Booklist*, 15 March 1988, 1244.

11. Diane Roback, review of *Beautiful Losers, Publishers Weekly*, 15 January 1988, 98.

12. Eleanor K. MacDonald, review of *Beautiful Losers*, *School Library Journal*, March 1988, 217.

13. Cathi Edgerton, review of *Beautiful Losers, Voice of Youth Advocates*, April 1988, 31.

5. Caring for Strays: The Tales of Heidi Rosenbloom

1. Barbara Wersba, *Just Be Gorgeous* (New York: Harper & Row, 1988), 28; hereafter cited in text by page number.

2. Barbara Wersba, *Wonderful Me* (New York: Harper & Row, 1989), 81; hereafter cited in text by page number.

3. Barbara Wersba, *The Farewell Kid* (New York: Harper & Row, 1990), 50; hereafter cited in text by page number.

4. This chapter's otherwise uncredited quotations and paraphrases from Wersba are from a telephone interview conducted by the author on 19 February 1996.

5. Hazel Rochman, review of *Just Be Gorgeous, Booklist*, 1 September 1988, 69.

6. Joanne Aswell, review of *Just Be Gorgeous, School Library Journal*, November 1988, 133.

7. American Library Association, "1991 ALA 'Best' Lists," *Booklist,* 15 March 1991, 1481.

6. Outrageous Adventures and Amazing Coincidences: The Best Place to Live Is the Ceiling, You'll Never Guess the End, *and* Life Is What Happens While You're Making Other Plans

1. Barbara Wersba, *The Best Place to Live Is the Ceiling* (New York: Harper & Row, 1990), 6; hereafter cited in text by page number.

2. This chapter's otherwise uncredited quotations and paraphrases from Wersba are from a telephone interview conducted by the author on 18 August 1996.

3. Diane Roback and Richard Donahue, review of *The Best Place to Live Is the Ceiling, Publishers Weekly*, 14 September 1990, 128; hereafter cited in text by page number.

4. Trev Jones, review of *The Best Place to Live Is the Ceiling, School Library Journal*, November 1990, 142.

5. Zena Sutherland, review of *The Best Place to Live Is the Ceiling, Bulletin of the Center for Children's Books*, January 1991, 132.

6. Susan Jelcich, review of *The Best Place to Live Is the Ceiling*, *Voice of Youth Advocates (VOYA)*, December 1990, 291.

7. Barbara Wersba, *You'll Never Guess the End* (New York: HarperCollins, 1992), 6; hereafter cited in text by page number.

8. Diane Roback and Richard Donahue, review of *You'll Never Guess the End*, *Publishers Weekly*, 12 October 1992, 80.

9. Janice Del Negro, review of *You'll Never Guess the End*, *Booklist*, 15 November 1992, 590.

10. Unsigned review of *You'll Never Guess the End*, *Kirkus Reviews*, 1 November 1992, 1386.

11. Barbara Wersba, *Life Is What Happens While You're Making Other Plans* (New York: The Bodley Head, 1994), 63; hereafter cited in text by page number.

12. Unsigned review of *Life Is What Happens While You're Making Other Plans*, *Junior Bookshelf*, February 1995.

7. *Seeking Solace:* Whistle Me Home

1. Barbara Wersba, *Whistle Me Home* (New York: Henry Holt, 1997), 15; hereafter cited in text by page number.

2. This chapter's otherwise uncredited quotations and paraphrases from Wersba are from a telephone interview conducted by the author on 4 October 1996.

3. Roger Sutton, review of *Whistle Me Home*, *Horn Book*, May/June 1997, 331; hereafter cited in text by page number.

4. Ilene Cooper, review of *Whistle Me Home*, *Booklist*, 1 April 1997, 1331.

5. American Library Association Young Adult Services (YALSA), "1998 Best Books for Young Adults," http://www.ala.org/yalsa/booklists/bestbooks98.html

6. American Library Association Young Adult Services Association (YALSA), "1998 Quick Picks for Young Adults," http://www.ala.org/yalsa/booklists/quickpicks98.html

7. Society for School Librarians International (SSLZ), "Book Awards, 1997–98, Language Arts 7–12 Novels

and Social Studies K–6," http://raven.jmu/~ramseyil/
sslibd.htm

**8. Here We Go Again!: Familiar Faces, Situations,
Places, and Themes**

1. After delivering a guest lecture on Barbara Wersba's
   work, at Hollins College in Roanoke, Virginia, I was
   asked why Barbara Wersba had not received the recognition she deserves as one of the first and enduring
   writers in the genre. My immediate response was,
   "Because she's too good." What follows in the text is a
   more reasoned version of the rest of the answer I gave
   that evening of 15 July 1996.

2. When her name is missing, as in Don Gallo's *Speaking
   for Ourselves* (Urbana, Ill.: National Council of Teachers of English [NCTE], 1990) and *Speaking for Ourselves, Too* (Urbana, Ill.: NCTE, 1993), it is not because
   she was not invited to contribute; she just choose not to
   accept the invitation.

Appendix

Awards and Honors

Books

The Carnival in My Mind: American Library Association Best Books for Young Adults, 1982; Cooperative Children's Book Center Choices, 1982.

The Country of the Heart: American Library Association Notable Children's Book, 1975.

Crazy Vanilla: Cooperative Children's Book Center Choices, 1986.

The Farewell Kid: American Library Association Books for Reluctant Readers, 1991.

The Dream Watcher: Library of Congress Children's Book Award, 1968; *Booklist* Junior Contemporary Classic, 1984.

Run Softly, Go Fast: American Library Association Best Books for Young Adults, 1970; German Juvenile Book Prize, 1973; American Library Association Best of the Best Books, 1968–1992.

Tunes for a Small Harmonica: American Library Association Best Books for Young Adults, 1976; American Library Association Notable Children's Book, 1976; National Book Award Finalist, Children's Book Category, 1977; National Council of Teachers of English Young Adult Book Poll of 1977 selection; *New York Times Book Review* Outstanding Children's Book, 1976.

Whistle Me Home: American Library Association Best Books for Young Adults, 1998; American Library Association Books for Reluctant Readers, 1998; Society of School Librarians International, Secondary Language Arts 7–12 Novel honor book, 1997.

Other

Honorary doctoral degree from Bard College, 1977.

Selected Bibliography

Primary Sources

Novels

The Dream Watcher. New York: Atheneum, 1968; Aladdin, 1968.

Run Softly, Go Fast. New York: Atheneum, 1970; Bantam, 1972.

The Country of the Heart. New York: Atheneum, 1975.

Tunes for a Small Harmonica. New York: Harper & Row ("An Ursula Nordstrom Book"), 1976.

The Carnival in My Mind. New York: Harper & Row ("A Charlotte Zolotow Book"), 1982.

Crazy Vanilla. New York: Harper & Row ("A Charlotte Zolotow Book"), 1986.

Fat: A Love Story. New York: Harper & Row ("A Charlotte Zolotow Book"), 1987; Dell Laurel-Leaf, 1988.

Love Is the Crooked Thing. New York: Harper & Row ("A Charlotte Zolotow Book"), 1987; Dell Laurel-Leaf, 1988.

Beautiful Losers. New York: Harper & Row ("A Charlotte Zolotow Book"), 1988; Dell Laurel-Leaf, 1989.

Just Be Gorgeous. New York: Harper & Row ("A Charlotte Zolotow Book"), 1988; Dell Laurel-Leaf, 1989.

Wonderful Me. New York: Harper & Row ("A Charlotte Zolotow Book"), 1989; Dell Laurel-Leaf, 1990.

The Best Place to Live Is the Ceiling. New York: Harper & Row ("A Charlotte Zolotow Book"), 1990.

The Farewell Kid. New York: Harper & Row ("A Charlotte Zolotow Book"), 1990; Dell Laurel-Leaf, 1991.

You'll Never Guess the End. New York: HarperCollins ("A Charlotte Zolotow Book"), 1992.

Life Is What Happens While You're Making Other Plans. London: The Bodley Head, 1994.

Whistle Me Home. New York: Henry Holt and Company, 1997.

Children's Books

The Boy Who Loved the Sea. Illustrated by Margot Tomes. New York: Coward-McCann, 1961.

The Brave Balloon of Benjamin Buckley. Drawings by Margot Tomes. New York: Atheneum, 1963.

The Land of Forgotten Beasts. Drawings by Margot Tomes. New York: Atheneum, 1964; London: Gollancz, 1965.

A Song for Clowns. Drawings by Mario Rivoli. New York: Atheneum, 1964; London: Gollancz, 1965.

Do Tigers Ever Bite Kings? Illustrated by Mario Rivoli. New York: Atheneum, 1966.

Let Me Fall Before I Fly. Frontispiece by Mercer Mayer. New York: Atheneum, 1971.

Amanda, Dreaming. Illustrated by Mercer Mayer. New York: Atheneum, 1973.

Twenty-six Starlings Will Fly Through Your Mind. Illustrated by David Palladini. New York: Harper & Row, 1980.

The Crystal Child. Drawings by Donna Diamond. New York: Harper & Row, 1982.

Retelling

The Wings of Courage, by George Sand. Retold by Barbara Wersba. New York: The Bookman Press, 1997.

Adaptations

The Dream Watcher. Play, adapted by Barbara Wersba, starring Eva Le Gallienne, first produced at White Barn Theatre, Westport, Connecticut, 29 August 1975; later produced by the Seattle Repertory Theatre, 1977–78.

Matters of the Heart. Television film starring Jane Seymour and produced by Martin Tahse. Adapted from Wersba's *The Country of the Heart*.

Essays and Tributes

"On Discovering Janet Frame." In *The Inward Sun: Celebrating the Life and Work of Janet Frame*. Edited by Elizabeth Alley, 163–65. Thorndon, New Zealand: Daphne Brasell Associates, 1994.

A Tribute to Zue Sharkey. New York: Bookman Press, 1994.

"Sexuality in Books for Children: An Exchange by Barbara Wersba and Josette Frank," *Library Journal,* 15 February 1973, 620–23.

"Barbara Wersba—as a Writer." *Top of the News,* June 1975, 427–28.

"Barbara Wersba." In *Literature for Today's Young Adults,* edited by Kenneth L. Donelson and Alleen Pace Nilsen, 443. Glenview, Ill.: Scott, Foresman and Company, 1980.

Secondary Sources

Books and Parts of Books

Commire, Anne, ed. *Something about the Author: Facts and Pictures about Authors and Illustrators of Books for Young People*. Detroit: Gale Research, 1990, 58:179–87.

Eaglen, Audrey. "Barbara Wersba." *Twentieth-Century Young Adult Writers*. Edited by Laura Standley Berger, 689–91. Detroit: St. James Press, 1994.

Garrett, Agnus and Helga P. McCue, eds. *Authors and Artists for Young Adults,* 2:235–43. Detroit: Gale Research, 1989.

Mercier, Jean F. "Barbara Wersba." In *Twentieth Century Children's Writers,* 2d ed. Edited by D. L. Kirkpatrick, 810–12. New York: St. Martins, 1983.

Sarkissian, Adele, ed. *Something about the Author Autobiography Series,* 2:293–304. Detroit: Gale Research, 1986.

Sieruta, Peter D. "Barbara Wersba." In *Children's Books and Their Creators*. Edited by Anita Silvey, 675. Boston: Houghton Mifflin, 1995.

Vandergrift, Kay. "Barbara Wersba." In *American Writers for Children since 1960: Fiction*. Edited by Glenn E. Estes, 52:374–79. Detroit: Gale Research, 1986.

Articles

Dannheiser, Grace. "Meet Barbara Wersba: An Actress Turns to Writing." *Rockland County Journal-News* (Nyack, N.Y.), 18 December 1968, 26.

Sherry, Linda. *"The Star* Talks To: Barbara Wersba." *East Hampton Star* (East Hampton, N.Y.), 29 January 1987, page number unknown.

"A Strange Girl's Wanderings." *Rockland County Journal-News* (Nyack, N.Y.). 24 October 1976, page number unknown.

Interviews

Janeczko, Paul. "Barbara Wersba." In *From Writers to Students: The Pleasures and Pains of Writing*. Edited by M. Jerry Weiss, 89–97. Newark, Del.: International Reading Association, 1970.

Janeczko, Paul. "An Interview with Barbara Wersba." *English Journal* 65 (November 1976): 20–21.

Selected Reviews: Novels

BEAUTIFUL LOSERS

Edgerton, Cathi. *Voice of Youth Advocates,* April 1988, 31.

Kirkus Reviews, 1 February 1988, 208.

MacDonald, Eleanor K. *School Library Journal,* March 1988, 217.

Roback, Diane. *Publishers Weekly,* 15 January 1988, 98.

Rochman, Hazel. *Booklist,* 15 March 1988, 244.

Sutherland, Zena. *Bulletin of the Center for Children's Books,* January 1988, 105.

Times Educational Supplement, 1 December 1989, 31.

Tucker, Nicholas. *Times Educational Supplement,* 6 May 1988, 28.

THE BEST PLACE TO LIVE IS THE CEILING

Cooper, Ilene. *Booklist,* 15 October 1990, 437, 440.

Jelcich, Susan. *Voice of Youth Advocates,* December 1990, 291–92.

Jones, Trev. *School Library Journal,* November 1990, 142.

Kirkus Reviews, 15 October 1990, 1461.

Poe, Elizabeth. *SIGNAL Newsletter,* Spring/Summer 1991, 26.

Publishers Weekly, 14 September 1990, 128.

Sutherland, Zena. *Bulletin of the Center for Children's Books,* January 1991, 132.

Webb, C. Anne. *ALAN Review,* Winter 1991, 21.

CARNIVAL IN MY MIND

Boehmer, Clare. *Catholic Library World,* September 1983, 91.

Booklist, 1 September 1982, 37.

Bulletin of the Center for Children's Books, October 1982, 39.

Forman, Jack. *School Library Journal,* September 1982, 145.

Greenlaw, M. Jean. *Journal of Reading,* December 1982, 276–77.

Heins, Paul. *Horn Book,* December 1982, 662–63.

McHargue, Georgess. "Coming of Age." *New York Times Book Review,* 14 November 1982, 2, 63.

Publishers Weekly, 1 October 1982, 127.

THE COUNTRY OF THE HEART

Catholic Library World, September 1976, 89.

Cosgrave, Mary Silva. *Horn Book,* December 1975, 618.

Harris, Karen. *School Library Journal,* September 1975, 128.

Gray, Mrs. John G. *Best Sellers,* December 1975, 299.

Kirkus Reviews, 1 July 1975, 719.

Matzner, Rosalind. "Love, Etc., in Young Adult Fiction, 1956–79." *Top of the News,* Fall 1980, 64.

McHargue, Georgess. "For Young Readers: Love and Death." *New York Times Book Review,* 4 January 1976, 4.

Nathan, Paul. *Publishers Weekly,* 25 November 1988, 27.

Publishers Weekly, 14 July 1975, 60.

"YA Best Books 1975." *Top of the News,* April 1976, 286.

CRAZY VANILLA

Clavin, Thomas. "Tyler in Sag Harbor." *Southampton Press,* 25 December 1986, B5.

Duncan, Marijo. *Voice of Youth Advocates,* December 1986, 223.

Gale, David. *School Library Journal,* November 1986, 109.

Jenkins, Christine. *Booklist,* 1 September 1990, 41.

Junior Bookshelf, April 1987, 95.

Kirkus Reviews, 1 November 1986, 1652–53.

Roback, Diane. *Publishers Weekly,* 26 December 1986, 57.

Sutherland, Zena. *Booklist,* 1 November 1986, 403.

Sutherland, Zena. *Bulletin of the Center for Children's Books,* March 1987, 137.

Vickery, Gill. *School Librarian,* May 1987, 160.

Waldron, Ann. *Philadelphia Inquirer,* 8 February 1987, 8.

THE DREAM WATCHER

Booklist and Subscription Books Bulletin, 1 November 1968, 304.

Bragg, Pamela. *Publishers Weekly,* 18 November 1968, 86.

"Dialogue Is Book's Chief Asset." *Rockland County Journal-News* (Nyack, N.Y.), 18 December 1968, 27.

Goodwin, Polly. "Book World." *Washington Post,* 3 November 1968, 18.

Haviland, Virginia, *Horn Book,* October 1968, 567.

Kirkus Reviews, 1 September 1968, 988.

Kirkus Reviews, 1 July 1975, 216–17.

Lewis, Naomi, "Books." *Observer,* 29 July 1990, 6.

Library Journal, 15 September 1968, 3328.

Parish, Maggie. "The Mother as Witch, Fairy Godmother, Survivor, or Victim in Contemporary Realistic Fiction for Young Adults." *English Journal,* October 1971, 101–103.

Peel, Marie. "Verges of Adulthood." *Books and Bookmen,* August 1969, 48.

Roth, Susan A. *School Library Journal,* 15 September 1968, 3328.

Saturday Review, 9 November 1968, 69.

Scanlon, Laura Polla. *Commonweal,* 22 November, 1968, 288–89.

Stavn, Diane Gersoni. "The Skirts in Fiction about Boys: In a Maxi Mess." *School Library Journal,* January 1971, 283.

Storr, Catherine. *New Statesman,* 31 October, 1968, 622–25.

"Time Listings." *Time* magazine, 13 December 1968, 2.

Times Literary Supplement, 26 June 1968, 686.

Watson, Jerry J. "A Positive Image of the Elderly in Literature for Children." *Reading Teacher,* April 1981, 792–97.

Weston, John. *New York Times Book Review,* Part 2, 3 November 1968, 2.

Young Readers' Review, November 1968, 13.

THE FAREWELL KID

Druse, Judy. *Voice of Youth Advocates,* October 1990, 222.

Kirkus Reviews, 1 March 1990, 348.

Kraar, Jennifer. *School Library Journal,* May 1990, 128.

Muller, Al. *ALAN Review,* Fall 1990, 25.

Perspectives, May 1991, 34.

"Recommended Books for the Reluctant Young Adult Reader, 1991."
Booklist, 15 March 1991, 1479–81.

Roback, Diane. *Publishers Weekly,* 16 March 1990, 72.

Rochman, Hazel. *Booklist,* 15 May 1990, 1793.

Sutherland, Zena. *Bulletin of the Center for Children's Books,* April 1990,
205.

FAT: A LOVE STORY

Booklist, 1 June 1987, 1517.

Burrington, Merilyn S. *School Library Journal,* August 1987, 99.

Children's Book Review Service, October 1987, 23.

Davidson, Andrea. *Voice of Youth Advocates,* June 1987, 84.

Kirkus Reviews, 1 July 1987, 1000.

Roback, Diane. *Publishers Weekly,* 12 June 1987, 86.

Sutherland, Zena. *Bulletin of the Center for Children's Books,* June 1987,
200.

Tucker, Nicholas. *Times Educational Supplement,* 6 May 1988, 28.

JUST BE GORGEOUS

Aswell, Joanne. *School Library Journal,* November 1988, 133–34.

Children's Book Review Service, October 1988, 24.

Culp, Mary Beth. *English Journal,* October 1991, 94.

Fakih, Kimberly Olson and Diane Roback. *Publishers Weekly,* 9 September 1988, 138, 140.

Jenkins, Christine. *Booklist,* 1 September 1990, 41.

Kirkus Reviews, 15 September 1988, 1141.

Publishers Weekly, 15 March 1991, 59.

Reece, Marguerite D. *Kliatt,* April 1991, 16.

Rochman, Hazel. *Booklist,* September 1988, 69.

Sasges, Judy. *Voice of Youth Advocates,* December 1988, 244.

Sutherland, Zena. *Bulletin of the Center for Children's Books,* December
1988, 111.

LIFE IS WHAT HAPPENS WHILE YOU'RE MAKING OTHER PLANS

Junior Bookshelf, February 1995.

King, Judy. *SIGNAL Journal,* Spring/Summer 1993, 31.

LOVE IS THE CROOKED THING

Andersen, Beth E. *Voice of Youth Advocates,* December 1987, 239.

Clavin, Thomas. "Novel Probes Teen Trauma." *Southampton Press,* 15
December, 1987, B1, B6.

Cooper, Ilene. "I've Never Been in Love Before: Romantic Comedies."
Booklist, 15 October 1990, 459.

Curley, Suzanne. "Sag Harbor Lovers, California Movers." *New York
Newsday,* 24 January 1988, 15.

Gerrard, Nicci. *New Statesman & Society,* 7 July 1989, 39.

Kirkus Reviews, 15 October 1987, 1524.

Locke, Deborah. *School Library Journal,* December 1987, 106.

Jantzen, Margaret Zinz. *Book Report,* March/April 1988, 37.

Roback, Diane. *Publishers Weekly,* 9 October 1987, 89–90.

Rochman, Hazel. "Books for Young Adults." *Booklist,* 1 October 1987, 255.

Sutherland, Zena. *Bulletin of the Center for Children's Books,* October 1987, 39.

Tucker, Nicholas. *Times Educational Supplement,* 6 May 1988, 28.

RUN SOFTLY, GO FAST

American Library Association. *Top of the News,* April 1971, 309.

Andrews, Sheryl B. *Horn Book,* December 1970, 624.

Booklist, 1 November 1970, 304.

Booklist, 1 April 1971, 655.

Catholic Library World, September 1976, 89.

Commonweal, 20 November 1970, 202.

Conner, John W. "Bookmarks." *English Journal,* April 1971, 530–31.

Donelson, Ken. "Fifty YA Books Out of the Past Still Worth Reading; or, Enjoyment Is There *If* You Search for It." *ALAN Review,* Fall 1986, 59–63.

Eble, Mary and Jeanne Renton. *Journal of Reading,* November 1978, 123–30.

Garden, Nancy. *American Observer,* 4 October 1971, page number unknown.

Leone, Angela. "Booksearch: Out-of-Print Books That Should Still Be in Print." *English Journal,* December 1991, 88–92.

Nilsen, Alleen Pace. "Books for Young Adults: Saying 'Hi' with Conviction: Books about Drugs," *English Journal,* May 1974, 89–91.

"Outstanding Books of the Year," *New York Times,* 8 November 1970, 34.

Poe, Elizabeth. *ALAN Review,* Fall 1993, 57–58.

Sutherland, Zena. *Bulletin of the Center for Children's Books,* February 1971, 100.

Sutton, Roger. "The Critical Myth: Realistic YA Novels." *School Library Journal,* November 1982, 33–35.

Thompson, Jean C. *School Library Journal,* 15 February, 1971, 738.

"Top One Hundred Countdown: Best of the Best Books for Young Adults." *Booklist,* 15 October 1994, 413.

Townsend, John Rowe. *New York Times,* 22 November 1970, 38.

TUNES FOR A SMALL HARMONICA

The Babbling Bookworm, February 1977, 3.

Booklist, 15 September 1976, 139 (starred review).

Carlsen, Robert G., Connie Bennett, and Ann Harker. "1977 Books for Young Adults Book Poll." *English Journal,* January 1978, 90–95.

Children's Literature in Education, February 1982, 77.

Churchill, David. *School Librarian,* June 1975, 165.
Commonweal, 19 November 1976, 763.
English Journal, January 1978, 92.
Flower, Ann A. *Horn Book,* December 1976, 631.
Growing Point, March 1979, 3486.
Haas, Diane. *School Library Journal,* Spring 1976, 127.
Junior Bookshelf, April 1979, 120.
Karlin, Barbara. "Kids." *West Coast Review of Books,* March 1977, 47.
Kirkus Reviews, 1 September 1976, 982–83.
Laski, Audrey. "The Problems of Being Different." *Times Educational Supplement,* 11 November 1983, 25–26.
Lazer, Ellen Abby. "Chronic Fantasies." *Book World—The Washington Post,* 10 October 1976, E6.
Matzner, Rosalind. "Love, Etc., in Young Adult Fiction, 1956–79." *Top of the News,* Fall 1980, 64.
Nelson, Alix. "Ah, Not to Be Sixteen Again." *New York Times Book Review,* 14 November 1976, 29, 52.
"Outstanding Children's Books of 1976." *New York Times Book Review,* 14 November 1976, 29.
Parish, Margaret. "The Mother as Witch, Fairy Godmother, Survivor, or Victim in Contemporary Realistic Fiction for Young Adults." *English Journal,* October 1979, 103.
Parish, Margaret. "Of Love and Sex and Death and Becoming and Other Journeys." *English Journal,* May 1978, 88–90.
Publishers Weekly, 12 July 1976, 72.
School Library Journal, November 1982, 34.
Stone, Rosemary. "Children's Books." *Books and Bookmen,* May 1986, 20.
Sutherland, Zena. *Bulletin of the Center for Children's Books,* Fall 1977, 99.
Vinson, Joe. *Best Sellers,* March 1977, 388.
Woods, George A. "Books for the Times: For Teens and Pre-Teens." *New York Times,* 21 December 1976, 31.

WHISTLE ME HOME
Cooper, Ilene. *Booklist,* 1 April 1997, 1331.
Poe, Elizabeth. *SIGNAL Journal,* Spring 1997, 33–34.
Sutton, Roger. *Horn Book,* May/June 1997, 331.

WONDERFUL ME
Druse, Judy. *Voice of Youth Advocates,* June 1989, 108.
Fakih, Kimberly Olsen and Diane Roback. *Publishers Weekly,* 13 January 1989, 92.
Marcus, Susan F. *School Library Journal,* April 1989, 120.
Purucker, Mary I. *Book Report,* November/December 1989, 48.
Rochman, Hazel. *Booklist,* 1 May 1989, 1540.
Sutherland, Zena. *Bulletin of the Center for Children's Books,* April 1989, 208.

Webb, C. Anne. *ALAN Review,* Fall 1989, 25.

YOU'LL NEVER GUESS THE END

Children's Book Review Service, 1992, 48.

Codell, Cindy Darling. *School Library Journal,* September 1992, 282.

Del Negro, Janice. *Booklist,* 15 November 1992, 590.

Hipple, Ted. *ALAN Review,* Spring 1993, 35.

Kirkus Reviews, 1 November 1992, 1386.

Roback, Diane and Richard Donahue. *Publishers Weekly,* 12 October 1992, 80.

Robertson, Joyce. *SIGNAL Newsletter,* Fall 1992, 31.

Voice of Youth Advocates, 2 April 1993, 4.

Selected Reviews: Children's Books

AMANDA, DREAMING

Babbitt, Natalie. *New York Times Book Review,* 7 October 1973, 8.

Hopkins, Lee Bennett. "Fantasy Flights circa 1976." *Teacher,* April 1976, 34.

McConnell, Ruth M. *Library Journal,* 15 February 1974, 567.

Publishers Weekly, 26 November 1973, 39.

THE BRAVE BALLOON OF BENJAMIN BUCKLEY

Pippett, Aileen. *New York Times Book Review,* 10 November 1963, 46.

THE CRYSTAL CHILD

Bulletin of the Center for Children's Books, July 1982, 219.

Language Arts, May 1983, 650.

Publishers Weekly, 16 July 1982, 79.

DO TIGERS EVER BITE KINGS?

Kirkus Reviews, 15 August 1966, 826.

Kluger, Richard. *Chicago Tribune Book Week,* 30 October 1966, 4–5.

Novak, Barbara. *New York Times Book Review,* 6 November 1966, 71.

Russ, Lavinia. *Publishers Weekly,* 29 August 1966, 344.

THE LAND OF FORGOTTEN BEASTS

Heins, Ethel L. *Horn Book,* October 1964, 499–500.

Leland, Dorothy. *Parents,* March 1965, 32.

L'Engle, Madeleine. *New York Times Book Review,* 25 October 1964, 36.

Times Literary Supplement, 9 December 1965, 1130.

Virginia Kirdus' Service, 15 July 1964. 651.

LET ME FALL BEFORE I FLY

Cunningham, Julia. "Notes for Another's Music." *Horn Book,* December 1971, 617.

Heins, Paul. *Horn Book,* December 1971, 616–17.

Orgel, Doris. *New York Times Book Review,* 17 October 1971, 8.

Publishers Weekly. 6 September 1971, 51.

A SONG FOR CLOWNS

Bodger, Joan H. *New York Times Book Review,* 21 November 1965, 56.

Heins, Ethel L. *Horn Book,* December 1965, 629–30.

Hurwitz, Joanna. *Library Journal,* 15 September 1965, 3797.

"One Foot on the Ground." *Times Literary Supplement,* 24 November 1966, 1087.

TWENTY-SIX STARLINGS

Bogstad, Janice M. "Is There Poetry in Children's Poetry?" *Lion and the Unicorn* 2.2 (1980): 83–92.

Children's Book Review Services, August 1980, 134.

Kennedy, X. L. *New York Times Book Review,* 9 November 1980, 62.

Language Arts, Fall 1981, 184.

Publishers Weekly, 8 August 1980, 83.

Index

Key

The Author

Elizabeth A. Poe is associate professor of English at Radford University, where she teaches undergraduate and graduate courses in young adult and children's literature. Before teaching at the college level, she taught secondary English for 13 years in Colorado. She is active in both the International Reading Association and National Council of Teachers of English special interest groups on young adult literature. She currently serves as editor of IRA's *SIGNAL Journal* and is a member of its Literature for Adolescents Committee, which oversees the Young Adults' Choices Project. She is a past president of NCTE's ALAN as well as the former book-review editor for the *ALAN Review* and coeditor of the "Now That You Asked . . ." column in that journal. She has also chaired the Colorado Blue Spruce Young Adult Book Award committee. Her publications include numerous book reviews, journal articles, book chapters, and teaching guides. She is the author of *Focus on Sexuality: A Reference Handbook* (Santa Barbara: ABC-CLIO, 1990) and coauthor of *Focus on Relationships: A Reference Handbook* (Santa Barbara: ABC-CLIO, 1993), informational books for teenagers that rely heavily on young adult fiction and nonfiction. She lives with her husband and twin teenage sons in Blacksburg, Virginia.

The Editor

Patricia J. Campbell is an author and critic specializing in books for young adults. She has taught adolescent literature at UCLA and is the former assistant coordinator of Young Adult Services for the Los Angeles Public Library. Her literary criticism has been published in the *New York Times Book Review* and many other journals. From 1978 to 1988 her column "The YA Perplex," a monthly review of young adult books, appeared in the *Wilson Library Bulletin*.

She now writes a column on controversial issues in adolescent literature for *Horn Book* magazine, "The Sand in the Oyster." Recently she has been traveling the country to lead her "YA Biblioramas," intensive workshops on young adult fiction for teachers and librarians.

Campbell is the author of five books, among them *Presenting Robert Cormier* (Boston: Twayne, 1989), the first volume in the Twayne Young Adult Author Series. In 1989 she was the recipient of the American Library Association Grolier Award for distinguished achievement with young people and books. A native of Los Angeles, Campbell now lives on an avocado ranch near San Diego, where she and her husband, David Shore, write and publish books on overseas motor-home travel.